The New Creative Serging Illustrated

The New Creative Serging Illustrated

The Complete Guide to Decorative Overlock Sewing

Pati Palmer , Gail Brown , Sue Green

Chilton Book Company
Radnor, Pennsylvania

Copyright © 1994, 1987 by Palmer/Pletsch Incorporated
Second Edition
All Rights Reserved
Published in Radnor, Pennsylvania 19089, by Wallace-Homestead,
a division of Chilton Book Company
No part of this book may be reproduced, transmitted, or stored
in any form or by any means, electronic or mechanical,
without prior written permission from the publisher.

Produced and designed by Read/Write Press.
Manufactured in the United States of America

Library of Congress Cataloging-in-Publication Data

Palmer, Pati
    The new creative serging illustrated : the complete guide to
decorative overlock sewing / Pati Palmer, Gail Brown, Sue Green. — 2nd ed.
        p. cm. — (Creative machine arts)
    Rev. ed of: Creative serging illustrated. ©1987.
    Includes index.
    ISBN 0-8019-8605-2 (hc); ISBN 0-8019-8382-7 (pb)
    1. Serging. I. Brown, Gail. II. Green, Sue. III. Palmer, Pati.
Creative serging illustrated. IV. Title. V. Series: Creative machine arts series.
TT713.P34   1994
646.2'044—dc20   93-38107
                                                                CIP

Photography by Carol Meyer; Palmer/Pletsch **Creative Serging** edition
design and production by Wisner Associates, Portland, Oregon; technical
and fashion illustrations by Kate Pryka; divider page fashion illustrations
by Diane Russell Kramer.

Contents

A Message From Robbie Fanning

The earlier version of this book appeared in 1987, when we had only a few books in the Creative Machine Arts series. Sergers were comparatively new and, compared to those of today, seem primitive. We've had lots of changes since 1987: We're now publishing four series with over 70 books out and lots more to come; and sergers have differential feed! beading feet! five threads!— and lots more to come.

But two things haven't changed: we love our sergers as much today as in 1987 and, as then, the team of Pati Palmer, Gail Brown and Sue Green still delivers a wallop of inspiration and ideas.

I am particularly energized by the new Serger Pro Showcase. Seeing those gorgeous clothes with all their decorative ideas and reading the helpful how-tos, makes me want to play hooky from work and play instead with my serger(s). And since I truly used and reused my copy of the first **Creative Serging Illustrated**, I'm happy that this version is in the larger format. It will stay open easier as it sits beside my machine.

Based on my experience during the six years between editions, I'd like to make some simple suggestions to make serging easier for you. I'm sure Pati, Gail, and Sue would concur. First, have at least one serger for each day of the week. Then you can work on rolled edges on one, flatlocking on another, etc., with a minimum of wasted effort. Secondly, have a live-in serger threader, as Bobbie Carr suggests. Finally, encourage the government to invest in serger research and development. The self-threading lower looper is already here. Think how much better your serging life would be if the power from jetting the thread through the lower looper also cleaned house and did the dishes. Is this too much to ask? I think not.

Robbie Fanning

Series Editor, *Creative Machine Arts* and co-author,
The New Complete Book of Machine Quilting

Acknowledgments

Several serger company representatives and freelance serger professionals took precious time out of their very busy schedules to lend garments, know-how and inspiration to the new "Serger Pro Showcase" beginning on page 51, and the chapter-divider illustrations: Marta Alto, Terri Burns, Cindy Cummins, Tammy Dunrud, Jonna Harris, Sue Hausman, Nel Howard, Marla Kazel, Eileen Lenniger, Paula Marineau, Agnes Merick, Judy Murphy, Phillip Pepper, Betty Quinell, Lynn Raasch, Cheryl Ribinson, Mary Sromek, Linnette Whicker, Kathy Wilkinson; also, the Singer Education Department and an Elna Educational Consultant.

We could not have written this book without the gracious cooperation of representatives from many sewing machine companies. Our special thanks to the following companies, listed in alphabetical order. (Please note that serger brand names often differ from the company names.)

Allyn International, 1075 Santa Fe Drive, Denver, CO 80204; Baby Lock U.S.A. (also known as Tacony), P.O. Box 730, Fenton, MO 63026; Bernina of America, 3500 Thayer Court, Aurora, IL 60504-6182; Brother International Corp., 8 Corporate Place, Piscataway, NJ 08854; Elna, Inc., 7642 Washington Ave. S., Eden Prairie, MN 55344; Juki Industries of America, Inc., 421 N. Midland Ave., Saddle Brook, NJ 07662 (or, on the West Coast, 3555 Lomita Blvd., Suite H, Torrance, CA 90505); New Home Sewing Machine Company, 100 Hollister Rd., Teterboro, NJ 07608; Pfaff American Sales Corp., 610 Winters Ave., Paramus, NJ 07653; Riccar America, 14281 Franklin Ave., Tustin, CA 92680; Sears, Sears Tower, Chicago, IL 60684; Simplicity Sewing Machines, P.O. Box 56, Carlstadt, NJ 07072; Singer Sewing Machine Co., 200 Metroplex Drive, P. O. Box 1909, Edison, NJ 0818-1909; Viking Sewing Machine Company, 11750 Berea Rd., Cleveland, OH 44111; White Sewing Machine Company, 11750 Berea Rd., Cleveland, OH 44111.

Also, a special thanks to Marta Alto and Lynn Raasch who have contributed so many tried-and-true serger ideas to Palmer/Pletsch. Over the years they have taught thousands of hands-on serger classes, and their contributions are based on experience. Also special thanks to Terri Burns who has added creativity and techniques to serging sweaterknits.

About the Authors

Gail Brown, a University of Washington Home Economics graduate, took her Clothing and Textiles degree to New York, where she became the marketing director for a fabric company. She has also been Communications Director for Stretch & Sew, Inc., and is a frequent guest on the "Sewing with Nancy" PBS television show. Her books include: **Sewing with Sergers**, **Sensational Silk**, **Sew a Beautiful Wedding**, **Innovative Serging**, **Innovative Sewing**, **Quick Napkin Creations**, **The Super Sweater Idea Book** and her latest title, **Gail Brown's All-New Instant Interiors**. In addition to her copywriting work for home-sewing companies, Gail's byline appears regularly in **Sew News** and **The Update Newsletters**. She is also an active participant on several online services, including America Online, CompuServe and Prodigy.

Sue Green has been a leading serger expert in the United States for several years. She entertains audiences with her light-hearted approach to this technical subject, not to mention that she can take apart and reassemble any serger! As former sewing machine and serger manager for a large fabric store chain, Sue was responsible for designing "how-to" lesson programs. As National Education Coordinator for one of the largest serger importers, she traveled the country conducting dealer training and consumer programs. She also developed serger workbooks and revised manuals. Sue writes for **Sew News** and **McCall's Pattern Magazine**. She was also an instructor for the four-day Palmer/Pletsch Serger Sewing Vacations held in Portland, Oregon.

Pati Palmer, President of Palmer/Pletsch Publishing, has been speaking to audiences throughout the U.S., Canada, and Australia for nearly 20 years. She has written or published nearly 20 books on sewing, fitting, and serging, including **Mother Pletsch's Painless Sewing**, **Pants for Any Body**, **Sewing Skinner Ultrasuede Fabric**, **Easier, Easiest Tailoring**, and **Sewing With Sergers**. Palmer/Pletsch initiated 4-Day Serger Vacations in Portland, Oregon in 1986. She has also taught hundreds of hands-on, one day workshops. Currently, her company offers teacher training to those wanting to use the Palmer/Pletsch format. In Pati's career she has worked as an educational representative for the Armo Company, as Corporate Home Economist for an Oregon department store, and as a notions buyer. She is a Home Economics graduate in Clothing and Textiles from Oregon State University where she was selected Oregon Home Economist of the Year in 1984. Pati is also Vice Chairman, Education for American Home Sewing and Craft Association and is on their board of directors. Among her other volunteer activities are in-coming chairwoman for the national organization of Home Economists in Business for which she was past National Public Relations Chairman and Vice-Chairman of Member Relations. She was also past Vice-Chairman of the Clothing and Textiles section of the American Home Economics Association. Pati has designed patterns for McCall's since 1980 and prior to that, for Vogue.

CHAPTER 1.
Introduction to Creative Serging

Creativity means originality, expressiveness, and imagination. Sergers give us decorative possibilities that open a whole new world of creativity for the home sewer...a creativity that looks sophisticated, not cutesy!

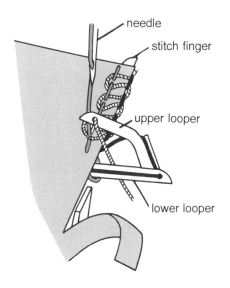

needle
stitch finger
upper looper
lower looper

A serger trims, then totally encases, an edge of fabric—unlike the zigzag on a conventional sewing machine. Also, because the stitches are formed over a metal stitch finger, the edge will never draw up, even on lightweight silkies. Because sergers have "loopers" that go **over** and **under** the fabric, heavy decorative threads, yarn, and ribbons can be used. These cannot be used on conventional machines because they will neither fit through the needle nor penetrate many fabrics.

What Is Decorative Serging?

Whenever serging shows, it is decorative...even when using regular thread. Serging will show **more** if you shorten the stitch length, use a contrasting color thread, a heavier thread, or a shinier thread like silk, rayon, or metallic. The following are decorative uses of a serger:

Exposed seams

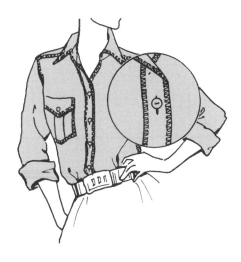

Satin stitched seam allowances that look like they are bound

Edges finished with a wide stitch

Rolled edges serged with matching or contrasting thread

Flatlocked seams

Heirloom sewing with laces and trims attached with serging

Our first book, **Sewing With Sergers**, covered serger basics. Since then, we've learned a lot more about the creative uses of a serger. Since we will help you be adventurous and experiment with many different ideas. Also, we can now help you **solve** nearly **every problem** you might encounter on your serger. Thanks to our four-day Palmer/Pletsch Serger Sewing Vacations held in Portland, Oregon, we've learned a lot. Be sure to see our **Serger Idea Book** for garment ideas and uses for the techniques in this book.

Make Your First Decorative Project Easy

For your first creative venture, choose one of the lighter weight decorative threads such as topstitching thread or Woolly Nylon and an easy-to-sew, inexpensive fabric such as polar fleece or sweatshirting. For ideas, see our chapter on creative sweatshirts.

The most important guideline for decorative serging is to **TEST** using a scrap of your garment fabric on the same grain. By adjusting the tension dials just a little, you can totally change the stitch or create a new one.

Child's decorative polar fleece coat

A creative sweatshirt

Once you've mastered decorative serging basics, graduate to heavier threads, yarns, and ribbons. Use this book to hold your hand as you become ULTRA CREATIVE. You won't believe how much fun you will have!

CHAPTER 2.
Serger Basics

The serger, also called an overlock machine, stitches, trims, and overcasts in one step at almost twice the speed of a conventional sewing machine. A conventional sewing machine sews from 700 to 1100 stitches per minute and a serger sews up to 1700 stitches per minute.

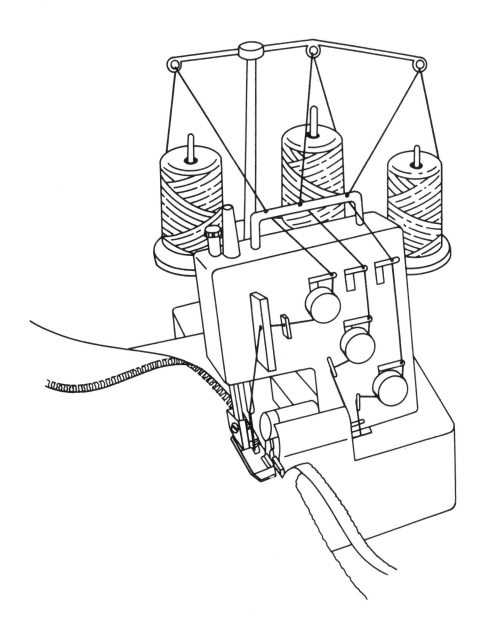

A 5–thread generic serger is illustrated here so that you can see the parts of a machine that has the maximum number of loopers and needles. For a 4–thread machine, just eliminate the left lower looper. For a 3–thread machine, eliminate one needle as well. On a 2–thread machine, there is only one needle and one looper.

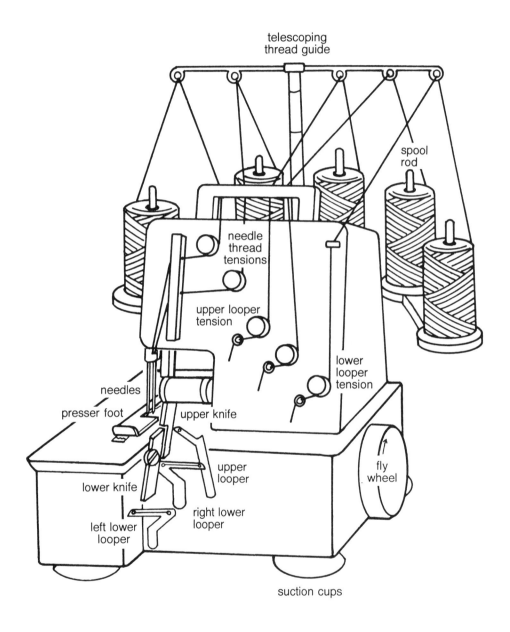

The Parts of a Serger

One important part of a serger that is very important to be aware of in decorative serging is what Sue lovingly calls "George." George is the extension on the back of the presser foot. Always put your threads **under** George before beginning to serge!

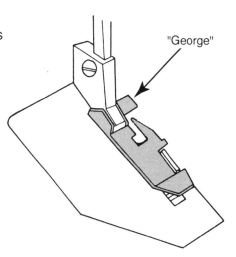

"George"

Sergers Have Improved

During the last 30 years, millions of sergers have been manufactured in Japan and Taiwan and sold to home sewers in this country. The growth curve has been steep—in 1976, only 20,000 sergers were imported to the U.S. compared to 600,000 in 1986. In fact, it is estimated that today, nearly one out of every four home-sewing households also owns a serger. With this increase in sales, has come technological improvements and many new features: built-in lights, external dials for adjusting stitch width and length, differential-feed capability, improved instruction books and videos, and now, even computerized stitch-selection panels. All of these contribute to our ability to use sergers creatively.

If you already own a serger, keep your first one even if you decide to upgrade. Today's luxury is having TWO sergers, like TWO cars! Keep one set up for regular seaming, and one for rolled edge or flatlocking.

How Are the Stitches Formed On Sergers?

The Stitch and Stitch Formation

2–Thread Overedge—formed in one of two ways:

The Over/Under Method: The upper looper goes over the top of the fabric, leaving a loop of thread that is caught by the needle. The upper looper goes under the fabric, picks up the needle thread and pulls it to the edge of the fabric. This method is found on "true" 4–thread and 2–thread machines that also do a chain stitch.

The Play Catch Method: You unthread and plug the upper looper, turning it into a "V"-shaped "hook." The lower looper goes under the fabric and hands a loop of thread to the upper looper which then places it on top of the fabric, ready to be caught by the needle. This method is used on machines that convert from 3–thread stitches; the upper looper goes back and forth over the top of the fabric only and cannot go over **and** under the fabric.

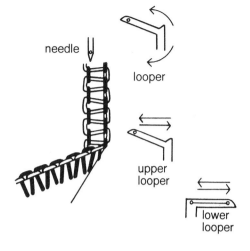

3–Thread Overlock—The threads connect or "lock" at the seam line, and the stitch looks approximately the same on both sides.

The upper looper goes over the top of the fabric leaving a loop which is caught by the needle.

The lower looper goes under the fabric, placing a loop of thread under the needle loop, then goes out to the edge where it knits together with the upper looper thread.

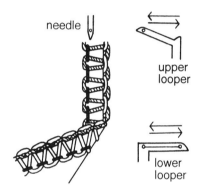

3/4–Thread Overlock—This is a 3–thread stitch with an extra needle thread running down the middle. Two types are available. In **A** leave out the left or right needle for a 3–thread stitch. In **B** leave out the left needle for a narrow 3–thread stitch. You must use both needles if you want a wide stitch.

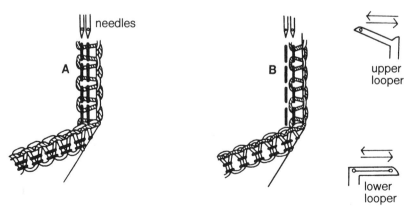

Stitch Characteristics and Uses

- Called an "overedge" stitch because the threads do not connect or "lock" at the seamline; therefore, it is not used to sew seams.
- Perfect if you primarily want to finish seam allowances and edges.
- With only two threads, seam and edge finishes are less bulky—nice for lightweight fabrics or when using heavier decorative threads.
- Flatlocking is easy and very flat with a 2–thread stitch.
- Some 2–thread machines can be adjusted to sew a rolled edge.
- There are 2–thread machines, but some 3–thread, all true 4–thread (chainstitch), and some 5–thread machines can convert to two threads.

    Note: One manufacturer used the term "seamlock" for a 2–thread seam. A strong seam can be sewn by tightening the needle tension all the way and loosening the looper tension. The needle thread then forms a straight line and the looper wraps the edge.

- Called an "overlock" stitch because the threads connect or "lock" at the seam line. Can be used to sew seams.
- Produces a balanced stitch that looks similar on both sides—great for reversibles.
- With three threads, seam and edge finishes can be slightly bulkier than with two threads because of the additional thread.
- Has lots of give, so is excellent for knits.
- Can be adjusted to sew a rolled edge.
- Ideal for decorative serging, especially if stitch width goes to 5mm or 7mm.
- Can be used a as a stable seam finish on loosely constructed, ravel-prone fabrics.

    Note: Some 3–thread machines can convert to two threads. Check your manual.

- A 3–thread overlock with the addition of an extra stitch down the middle for added durability.
- All four threads are not necessary for a serged seam.
- Excellent for clothes that get hard wear and/or frequent washings, like sportswear, childrenswear, and menswear.
- Has as much give as a 3–thread stitch.
- Interesting decorative effects created when different color threads are used in the needles and loopers.
- 3/4–thread machines can flatlock with one or both needles.
- On some 3/4–thread sergers the stitch width can be changed only by eliminating a needle, while on others, the stitch width is variable by adjusting the movable knife position (also known as the "bite").

    Note: Several manufacturers now offer 2/3/4–thread machines and 5–thread machines that are capable of serging a 3/4–thread stitch (in addition to others).

True 4–thread—a chainstitch combined with a 2–thread overedge:

The chainstitch—the left needle and the lower looper form a 2–thread chain stitch.

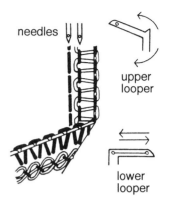

The 2–thread overedge—The right needle and the upper looper form the 2–thread overedge stitch constructed as described on page 8.

All **4** threads are needed to sew a serged **seam**.

5–thread Stitch—a chainstitch combined with a 3–thread overlock:

The chain—the left needle and left lower looper form a 2–thread chainstitch.

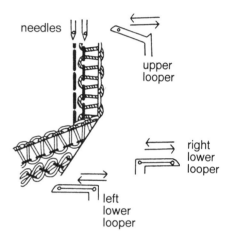

3–thread overlock—formed as described on page 8.

Conversion option: The 3–thread overlock on many 5–thread machines can be converted to a 2–thread overedge. The chainstitch plus overedge LOOK LIKE a "true" 4–thread stitch, but is formed differently.

Some machines give you the option of a 3/4–thread stitch as well.

The chainstitch—formed as described above.

The 2–thread overedge—formed using the play catch method described on page 8.

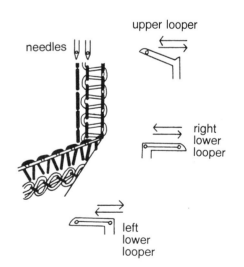

Stitch Characteristics and Uses

- Made up of a 2–thread chainstitch and a 2–thread overedge stitch. All four threads are necessary to sew a serge seam.

- Well-suited for ravelly, loosely woven fabrics because the chain forms a strong seam and the seam allowance is wider.

- The seam is also wide enough to press flat and create an even topstitch.
- It has less stretch than a 3–thread stitch so it can stabiles stretchy areas.

- Used whenever a wider seam allowance is desirable for strength (upholstery) or when a seam needs to be pressed flat (jackets, slacks).

- Some 4/2–thread machines can sew a rolled edge.

- Sews a 2–thread chainstitch in combination with a 2–thread overedge or a 3–thread overlock stitch.

- A chainstitch, 2–thread overedge, 3–thread overlock or optional 3/4–thread overlock can each be used independently.

- By using the 2–thread chainstitch and 3–thread overlock stitch together, the seam is very durable.

- Use the 3–thread overlock stitch alone for seams that require stretch.

- Can sew rolled edges with either 2–thread or 3–thread stitch.

- A very wide (up to 9mm) seam width is created when the chain is serged with either the 2– or 3–thread stitch. Great for durability, particularly on wovens.

- Some chainstitches can be serged within the project, for topstitching—any distance from the edge and without cutting. Others are limited to seaming, with seams being only as wide as the maximum stitch width.

CHAPTER 3.
Updated Decorative Thread Glossary

Use this chapter as a reference when choosing and serging with the latest decorative threads, yarns, and ribbons. We've listed them in order of serging difficulty, starting with the easiest. At the end of the chapter we've summarized tension tips for each type in a handy, quick-reference chart.

Regular Thread

Chose extra-fine, serger, or all-purpose thread. The latter is the heaviest, yet the difference is subtle. One advantage of using these three types of thread decoratively is that you can use them in the needle as well as the loopers. Also, all-purpose thread is available in a wide range of colors.

For better coverage when decoratively serging, we recommend a short stitch length for regular thread, especially on the edge of a woven fabric. We call a short stitch a "satin" stitch. With knits or non-wovens, you can use a longer stitch length if a more open look is desired.

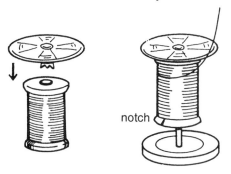

notch

For conventional spools, use the cap that comes with your machine to help the thread reel off quickly and evenly. Place the cap on the spool or the rod. (Check your manual.) Place the notched side of the spool down.

Creative Uses:

* Lapped seams and edges on a shirt

* Lightweight rolled edges on a full skirt hem

* Lapped seams on synthetic suede

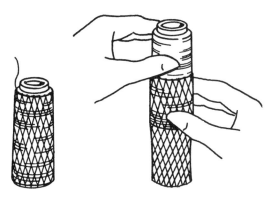

Nylon Monofilament Thread

Some ready-to-wear manufacturers use this translucent thread in their general sewing so they don't need to change thread every time they change fabric color. It automatically "matches" the fabric. Most of the newer nylon threads are fine, soft, and not wiry, such as the new #80, #60 and .004 weights. Nylon thread can be used in the needle as well as in both loopers. Tension settings are generally normal. You may need to cover the spool with netting to prevent spilling or slipping off the spool.

Try using nylon filament thread in the lower looper of a rolled edge stitch. It stretches slightly while feeding through the machine and can help tighten the lower looper for a nice rolled edge.
One of our favorite uses of nylon filament thread is in the needle and **lower** looper. Use a heavy decorative thread, yarn, or ribbon in the **upper** looper. The "invisible" nylon makes the upper looper thread appear as if it is just floating on the surface of the fabric.

Topstitching Thread

A highly twisted, cord-like polyester or cotton-covered polyester thread often called buttonhole twist. It covers an edge better than regular thread and is available in many colors.

Topstitching thread can be used in the needle(s) as well as the loopers. Use a spool cap because the thread tends to embed itself on the spool. The wide angle created by the spool cap (page 13) helps the thread flow freely.

We love the versatility and ease of topstitching thread, and are delighted that some manufacturers now sell more yardage on a spool, such as Jeans Stitch from Y.L.I. (150 meters/spool). If using smaller yardage spools, however, make sure you have enough thread to complete an entire project. See page 13 for estimating yardage. If you do run short, see page 13 for repair tips. If it only comes in a small spool, we suggest buying one **just for testing**.

Note: New high-sheen acrylic topstitching threads, such as Decorative Thread from New Home, serge smoothly and trouble-free, too.

Creative Uses:

- Flatlocked and fringed challis scarves

- Edges of coats and jackets that are serged rather than stitched and turned

- Wonderful for rolled edges on napkins as it washes well

- Decorative stitching on synthetic suedes and leathers

- Flatlocking on sweatshirts and actionwear (washes well)

Rayon Thread

Looks similar to silk, with its beautiful sheen, but much less costly. It is available in fine, medium, and heavy weights, the most prevalent being a weight about halfway between regular and topstitching thread.

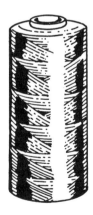

Rayon thread is primarily used in the upper looper. It tends to break easily when used in the needle and lower looper due to friction. Because it also slips through the tension discs easily due to its slickness, you might need to tighten the tensions slightly. Serge a test sample. For rolled edges we recommend it only in the upper looper. The lower looper needs to be tightened and slippery thread pass through freely. In other words, you may not be able to get a tight enough lower looper with rayon thread. It is available on cones and spools and netting might be needed to keep it from spilling.

Rayon thread is colorfast and washable, and comes in a wide range of very intense colors including variegated shades. Available brands include Madeira, Natesh, Sulky, Y.L.I., and Pfaff's new MEZ Alcazar.

There are also some lovely, heavier rayon threads. Decor 6 is an untwisted filament thread. Designer 6 is a slightly twisted filament thread for shine with added durability. And Pearl Crown Rayon is a twisted rayon thread with the most durability but the least amount of shine. All are colorfast and washable. Although they can be used in both loopers, you will have the most success using them in the needle as well as upper looper.

Creative Uses:

- Wide, shiny satin stitch on the edge of Chanel-style jackets (resembles trim)

- Rolled edges on scarves

- Medium width satin stitch in unlined jackets to resemble a silky Hong Kong seam finish

- Shiny rolled edge seams in heirloom sewing

Silk Thread

Similar to rayon in look and stitching characteristics, but with a color and sheen unique to only silk (and a more expensive price tag to match). Both Things Japanese and Y.L.I. sell imported silk threads, in a range of weights; ask for them in stores that specialize in silks and/or decorative stitchery. Topstitching weight comes on spools with a small amount of yardage.

Woolly Nylon

In 1984, Y.L.I. introduced its Woolly Nylon to the home sewing market. It is a heat-set, texturized or crimped, thread that looks fuzzy like wool. It is about the same weight as regular sewing thread; however, because it is lofty and not twisted, it spreads to cover an edge. Y.L.I.'s product is now available in metallic and variegated shades. Similar products are Bulky Lock from Coats, Metroflock by Swiss-Metrosene, S-T-R-E-T-C-H-Y by Corticelli, and Designer Edge by Talon.

These threads can be used in the needle as well as the loopers. We find it necessary to loosen tensions considerably to allow this thread to flow without too much stretching. It is one of the strongest threads for its weight, therefore it is perfect for activewear. It also can be sewn using a very short stitch length for great coverage on the raw edge of a woven fabric. It should not be ironed with a hot iron due to its heat sensitivity.

Creative Uses:

- Edges of a single-layer wool cape, since it can be used in both loopers for complete reversibility.

- Edges of placemats—good "coverage," washable, and prevents corners from ravelling

- Edge finishing in ravelly fabrics or seams in activewear where strength is essential

Metallic Thread

There is a difference among brands. Some are very fine, resembling silk, while others are coarse and metal-like. Your choice depends on the look you want. Metallics work best in the upper looper. Some will strip back or fray when used in the needle or lower looper. Test first!

Use gold or grey regular thread in the needle to blend with gold or silver metallics. With a shorter stitch length, the coarser metallics lay at random. They don't look as smooth and even as the finer metallics. Try tightening the tensions slightly to smooth them out. Some may look better with a long stitch length. They come on cones, tubes and spools. Or, try metallic Woolly Nylon—it sews beautifully. The heavier metallic yarns such as Y.L.I's Candlelight (now available on 500-yard tubes) and Madeira's Glamour sew beautifully and offer excellent coverage. Also, consider economical metallic needlepunch yarns.

Creative Uses:

• Rolled edges on holiday napkins

• A wide satin stitch on edges of placemats

• The neckline of a sweaterknit using a wide width

• Pintucks on an evening blouse

• Ruffles on sheers

• Dancewear

• Fancy scarf edges

• Dramatic touch on a basic black or white dress

Crochet Thread

Available in cotton or acrylic fibers and in many colors. The cotton variety, a highly twisted, mercerized thread, is slightly thicker than topstitching thread. It is strong and easy to use in upper as well as lower loopers, but too thick for the needle. The acrylic variety (Burmilana by Madeira) is similar to cotton only slightly fuzzier, hence a perfect coordinate for wools and sweater knits. Coats & Clark is a major manufacturer of crochet threads, and their Knit-Cro-Sheen is available in both cotton and acrylic. Crochet thread is wound on balls that average 175 yards each. DMC is another manufacturer of crochet thread. See pages 23 and 29 for hand-feeding and tension tips.

Creative Uses:

• Gail sewed a single layer jacket without facings using upholstery fabric. She used acrylic crochet thread in both loopers to finish the outside edges, making the jacket reversible.

• Edges of quilted placemats

• Edges of thick fuzzy woolens to create your own blankets and throws

Pearl Cotton

A mercerized 100% cotton that is shiny, soft, and not highly twisted. Two widely distributed sizes are #8 (finer) and #5 (thicker). It is available in 50-yard balls or smaller, 10-yard skeins. Also, Dual Duty Pearl Cotton is available on 150-yard cones that are ideal for the serger. Pearl cotton comes in a wide variety of colors including interesting variegated shades.

Our preference is to use pearl cotton in the upper looper. You can use it in the lower looper, but the extra thread guides can cause fraying. Also, because of the loose twist, the needle can split the pearl cotton as it is "thrown" over the top of the fabric by the upper looper. Serging slowly will generally solve this problem. If using pearl cotton wound on a ball, see pages 23 and 29 for hand-feeding and tension tips.

Creative Uses:

- Flatlocked fringe on a wool challis scarf

- Edges of a cotton interlock knit in a sporty jumpsuit using a bright contrast color

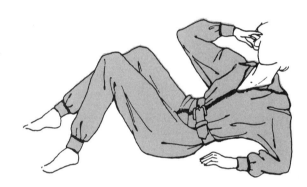

- Edges of baby clothes and receiving blankets using a variegated pastel color

Yarn

The key to successfully serging with yarn is to use one that is fine, strong, tightly twisted, and smooth. To test for adequate strength, pull on a strand. If it breaks easily, it will also break easily when serging. If it is too loosely twisted, it can be caught by the needle and jam your machine. If it's too lumpy, it won't flow evenly.

Easy to use—a fine, even, tightly twisted yarn

Difficult to use—a thick, slubby, untwisted yarn

We've had good luck with baby yarn (it comes in pastel and variegated shades), as well as sock or sweater yarn (it comes in neutral colors). Both are fine, strong, and twisted enough for smooth feeding. Sport or "fingering" weight yarns are available in a wider color range, but each brand and fiber varies, so first test serge on scraps. Also, acrylic needlepunch yarns serge easily, and are widely distributed in a broad color range.

Keep fiber content in mind, too. Acrylic yarn works well because it is very strong. Wool yarn is weaker, but twisting the plies can add strength. Blending wool with nylon also helps. You can try cotton and silk yarns; however, we've found that they can lack the resiliency and drape necessary for hiccup-free serging.

Note: For a strong, sergeable wool yarn, try Sew-Art International's Renaissance Thread. Designed for machine embroidery, it's fine enough to use in both the needle(s) and looper(s). Yarn is generally used in the upper looper only. The extra thread guides in the lower looper can cause fraying. See page 23 for feeding tips and page 29 for tension tips.

Creative Uses:

- Variegated pastel yarn on edges of a double-layer, receiving blanket

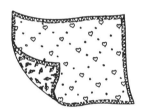

- Edges of a boiled wool jacket

- Edges of a single-layer wool cape

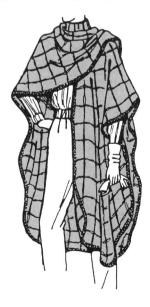

- Neckline, sleeve, and bottom edges of a sweater

Ribbon

Soft knitting ribbon 1/6" to 1/4" wide works well in the upper looper of a 3–thread and the looper of a 2–thread serger. See pages 23 and 29 for feeding and tension tips. Y.L.I. is one of the manor distributors of decorative knitting ribbons. The following are available.

Silk Ribbon—Expensive, but can be purchased by the yard, rather than by the spool. See page 23 for estimating yardage.

Rayon Ribbon—Very shiny, drapable, and soft like silk. These new braided ribbons are durable, and work in both loopers. Look for Ribbon Floss, Ribbon Thread, or Tinsel Twill ribbon.

Acrylic Ribbon—Very shiny, drapable, and soft like silk, but less expensive. Often called synthetic silk.

Cotton Ribbon—Durable and washable. Great as a trim for children's clothes. Choose a very fine, soft type for easiest sewing.

Polyester Ribbon—Generally too stiff, but worth a test.

Creative Uses:

• Edges of ruffles for childrenswear and frou-frou blouses

• Edges of sweaterknits—the combination of textures is lovely

• As part of an heirloom serging scheme, add a row or two of ribbon serging

Decorative Thread, Yarn, and Ribbon Guide

The next chapter goes into detail on handling decorative thread, yarn, and ribbon; however, use this handy chart for quick reference.

Thread	Needle(s)	Upper Looper	Lower Looper	Tension
Clear Nylon	Yes	Yes	Yes	Normal
Topstitching	Yes	Yes	Yes	Slightly looser
Rayon	Can break	Yes	Can break	Tighten
Woolly Nylon	Yes	Yes	Yes	Loosen
Metallic	May fray	Yes	May fray	Normal, Test May require some loosening
Crochet	Too thick	Yes	Sometimes	Loosen a lot
Pearl Cotton	Too thick	Yes	Sometimes	May need to loosen or remove completely from tension disc and/or thread guides
Yarn	Too thick	Yes	Sometimes	
Ribbon (silky)	Too thick	Yes	Sometimes	

CHAPTER 4.

The Best Decorative Basics

Read this chapter before you begin decorative serging and you will avoid lots of frustration. Decorative serging is very creative, but you are pushing your serger to do more than its basic functions. With patience, you will be able to create looks you've never before thought possible. You'll really have a one-of-a-kind garment!

Where to Use Decorative Threads on Your Serger

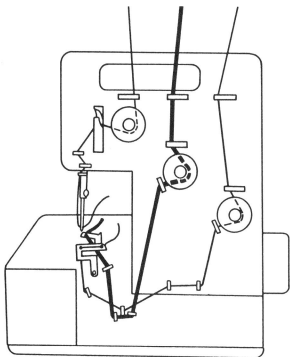

Generally, we use heavier decorative threads in the **upper looper**. There are fewer thread guides, so less stress is exerted on the thread. The lower looper has two holes and more thread guides causing stress and thread breakage.

Lighter weight decorative threads can be used anywhere, even in the needle. Make sure the needle is large enough to accommodate the thread, yet not so large that it damages the fabric. We use a size 14 needle for topstitching thread and an 11 or 12 needle for regular thread.

Note: For those sergers that use household needle(s), the new "Metallic" needles (with larger eyes and specially designed sergers) work well with decorative threads.

Threading Tips

- **Thread in proper order**—Check your manual for recommended order. In our first book we started with the lower looper, but since the upper looper thread guides are usually **behind** the lower looper thread guides, it may be easier to begin with the upper looper, then thread the lower looper and finally the needle.

- **All guides must be threaded!**—Missing a guide is the number one cause of stitching problems on a serger. Always DOUBLE CHECK the guides.

- Make sure the looper threads aren't tangled or they will break!

Good
Totally
separate

Good
Lower looper thread
over upper looper thread

Disaster
Lower looper thread
between upper looper
and upper looper thread

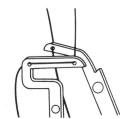
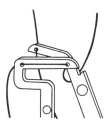

- **Don't use too heavy thread, yarn, or ribbon**—As a rule of thumb, if you have to **force** a double layer of decorative thread through the looper, it is **too** heavy to use on your machine.

- **There is an easy way to get a heavy thread through a small hole**—You can bend or break the looper threader that comes with some machines if you use it with heavy threads.

Instead, form a thread "cradle." Cut twelve inches of regular thread and wrap it around your heavier thread forming a loop. Then thread both ends of the regular thread through the looper hole. Use tweezers if necessary. Pull the heavier thread through the hole. You can also use a looper threader (see page 150).

- **Be sure threads are engaged in tension discs**—Tug on thread just above and below the tension discs to make sure they are engaged. You should feel resistance on each thread.

- **After threading, "clear" threads before beginning to stitch**.

If you turn the flywheel around while threading, the needle thread will wrap around the lower looper causing breakage.

To prevent this problem, slide a seam ripper or similar tool under the presser foot to draw up the needle thread.

How Much Decorative Thread Will I Need?

It is frustrating to run out of thread. To estimate what is needed, Sue serged one yard of fabric with five types of decorative threads, yarns, and ribbons. Then she measured the amount used. Her stitch length was 2.5mm and width 5.0mm. She found the following:

Thread	Yards per looper needed to sew one yard of fabric (varies with stitch length and width used)
Pearl cotton	6-1/2 yards
Topstitching thread	7 yards
Crochet thread	8 yards
Sport yarn	5-1/2 yards
1/8" ribbon	7-1/2 yards

(P.S. For our friends on the metric system, we have included a conversion chart in the back of the book.)

Add to these amounts one yard for threading the machine and at least ten yards for testing. Of course, if you change your stitch length and width, the amounts given in the chart will vary.

You may wonder why more crochet thread is used than ribbon. It is because crochet thread is wiry and lies on the fabric in a neat, rounded "S" pattern. Ribbon is softer and folds over on top of itself; therefore, less is used. Why is so much less yarn used? Yarn stretches or elongates as it goes through the machine.

Reel Off By Hand When Using Skeins or Balls

If your decorative thread, yarn, or ribbon is not wound on spools, you must make sure it **feeds freely** as you serge. Any restriction on the thread will cause uneven stitching.

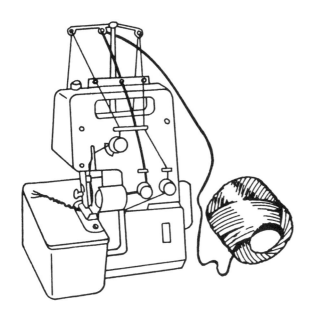

At first, we rewound thread from balls and skeins onto an empty cone or spool, but found it added tension to the thread. We now recommend placing the ball or skein on its side on the table next to the machine, in a bowl, or on the floor. Then reel off a large quantity and serge—reel and serge—reel and serge. Just don't forget to keep reeling so there is plenty of slack between the ball or skein and the first thread guide.

Always Test First!

It's difficult to correct a mistake. Pati learned the hard way. Her round-neck top grew into a "U"-neck style, because she forgot to test. After all, the **easiest** way to correct a problem is to cut away your mistake.

You will need a 30" length of fabric for thorough testing. Test on the same grain you'll be sewing. A **long** strip of fabric allows you to serge 5", stop and look at both sides, adjust tensions if necessary, and serge another 5". Do this until you achieve the look desired.

Serge Slowly

We can't emphasize enough the importance of sewing **slowly**. Even though your serger was made for speed, heavier threads pose a variety of potential problems. Fast serging can cause the looper threads to tangle and the power of the motor can cause the tangled threads to bend the loopers. Also, if you serge too fast, extra tension will be placed on the thread and cause uneven stitching.

Stitch Width

A wider stitch shows off the decorative thread better. We recommend beginning your TEST sample with the widest stitch and narrowing it a little at a time until you achieve the look you want.

Stitch Length

Begin serging your TEST sample with the **longest** stitch possible to prevent jamming under the presser foot. Hold on to your tail chain when you begin. Gradually shorten the stitch length until the desired look is achieved. Remember, "fatter" threads take up more room (as shown in our example) even though the stitch length is the same.

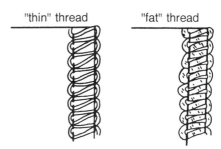

"thin" thread   "fat" thread

Steps to Headache-Free Decorative Serging

After threading the machine, use the following order for TEST sewing:

1. Set the stitch length and width according to the above instructions.

2. Rotate the handwheel **in the correct direction** by hand. See if the stitches are forming on the stitch finger.

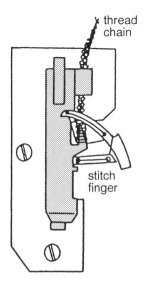

thread chain

stitch finger

3. It is not always necessary to lift the presser foot during regular serging. However, you MUST LIFT the presser foot and place the fabric under it when using decorative threads. It helps begin the "feeding" and prevent jamming. If the needle is up, the knives are open so you can place the fabric right into the knife jaws.

4. Always, at least, **skim** the fabric edge with the knives for even width stitches, even if not trimming away any seam allowance.

5. Begin sewing SLOWLY! Check your stitches every five inches.

Your Thread Breaks During Testing

If one of your threads breaks during testing, try the following:

1. Double-check to see if the machine is threaded correctly.

2. Check to see if the threads are caught in the spool's notch.

3. Check to see if all threads are engaged in tension discs.

4. Try loosening the tension on the thread that broke.

5. If all else fails, rethread the machine from scratch!

6. It still breaks? Rethread the machine with regular thread in order to determine whether you have a mechanical problem or your thread just doesn't like that particular decorative thread.

Everything You Ever Wanted to Know About Tension

Every serger has tension dials. Sue prefers not to use this term. It reminds her of tension head-aches! Instead, she call them "stitch formers." And that is really what they are. Even a slight tension change can alter the look of the stitch. In decorative serging, there is no RIGHT or WRONG tension—whatever tension achieves the look desired is the correct tension.

Note: See our first book, **Sewing with Sergers, Revised**, for in-depth tension diagrams for all types of stitches.

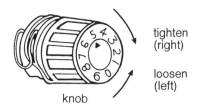

tighten
(right)

loosen
(left)

knob

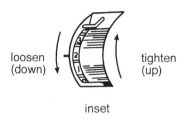

loosen
(down)

tighten
(up)

inset

Tension dials are mounted on the outside or set into the machine. Gail's favorite way of remembering which way to turn the dial is a saying: "RIGHTY, TIGHTY and LEFTY, LOOSEY." Silly as it sounds, you won't forget it.

This doesn't work for vertical built-in or inset dials. We suggest looking at your manual and putting arrows on your machine with masking tape for quick reference. Generally, the bigger the numbers, the tighter the tension. Try remembering UP, TIGHT for tightening if that works for your machine. Also, now some are marked with an "N" for normal and a "+" for tightening or "-" for loosening.

Which Dial Controls Which Thread?

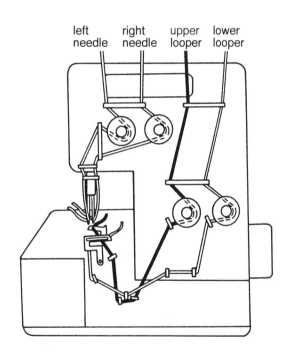

left
needle

right
needle

upper
looper

lower
looper

How about another rule? When there are four dials, the top two are for the needles and the lower two are for the loopers. The top left is for the left needle and the right for the right needle. If the two lower ones are at the same level, the one on the left is the upper looper and the one on the right is the lower looper.

Mark them with masking tape until you can quickly remember their function. Since "rules" are often broken, so is this one. Some recent models are moving their tension dials to different places. Also, 5–thread models have two lower looper dials for a left lower looper and right lower looper (see page 41).

The Secret to Correcting Tension Problems

Don't turn more than one dial at a time. Adjust the dial that appears too tight first, then TEST SEW. If the looper threads are unbalanced, do the same. Loosen the tight one first. If that doesn't solve the problem, return that dial to its original position and tighten the one that appears too loose. How do you know which is too tight? Read on!

How to Recognize Tension Problems

Diagnosis of tension problems is easy if you know what to look for. Remember the following:

1. The needle tension dial controls the **seam line**.

2. The upper looper tension dial controls the **top** side of the overcast.

3. The lower looper tension dial controls the **under** side of the overcast.

If your seam is pulling apart
like this...

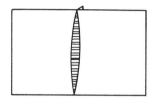

...tighten the needle tension.

knob   inset

If your seam puckers
like this...

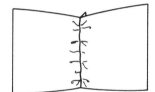

...loosen the needle tension

knob   inset

If your stitch looks like this,
loosen the upper looper and/or
tighten the lower looper.

If your stitch looks like this,
loosen the lower looper and/or
tighten the upper looper.

loosen

U.L.   U.L.

tighten

U.L.

tighten

L.L.   L.L.

knob   inset

loosen

L.L.   L.L.

knob   inset

Heavy Decorative Threads Break Tension Rules

To get a **balanced** stitch, each tension dial will be set at a different place when using a thick thread in one looper and a thin thread in the other. You will need to ignore the recommended settings in your manual.

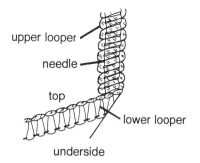

upper looper
needle
top
lower looper
underside

The reason is that heavier threads create more **resistance** in the tension dials. A fatter thread simply **takes up more room**.

Decrease tension for thicker threads.

Increase tension for thinner threads

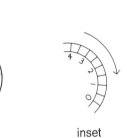

knob   inset

knob   inset

If you loosen the tension on heavy thread completely and it is still too tight, try removing the thread from one or more thread guides. If that doesn't work, completely remove the thread from the tension dial as shown. **Experiment!**

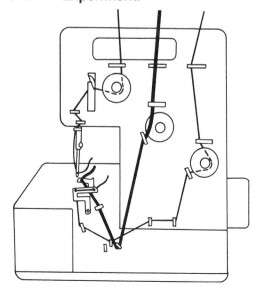

If your machine has a "squeezie" guide at the top, remove the thread from it first.

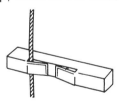

If your serger has "lay-in" dials, cover the dial with masking tape to keep thread out of tension discs.

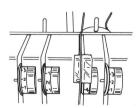

Our Best Tension Tip of All

After teaching several four-day workshops, we discovered the obvious. The WIDTH of the loops is controlled by tension. **Looper** width can be changed by loosening or tightening tension.

In this drawing of a balanced stitch, the loops hug the edge of the fabric.

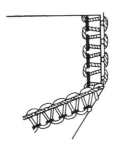

Here, we've loosened the looper tensions. The loops widen and hang over the edge of the fabric.

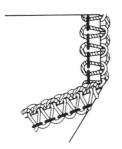

If you actually **change stitch width**, you will move the needle or knife blades. In addition, you will need to change the tensions as follows:

The **wider** the stitch, the **more** looper thread you'll need. Loosen both looper tensions and let more thread flow through.

The **narrower** the stitch, the **less** thread you'll need. Tighten the tension dials to let less thread flow through.

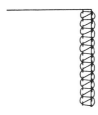

If you **widen** the stitch without loosening the tension, you may get the "pokies" on a woven fabric. The loops are too tight (narrow) against the edge. Loosen the looper tensions.

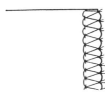

If you **narrow** the stitch width without tightening the tension, you can get "sloppy" loops or they might hang over the edge too far. Tighten the looper tensions.

When tension is **unbalanced**, a wide loop might even wrap over the edge. Often it is "pulled" over the edge by a narrow loop. Look at the following examples. Which loops need to be narrower? Which ones need to be wider? Always loosen the one that's too tight first!

Loosen (widen) the lower looper tension. You may then need to tighten the upper looper tension.

Loosen the upper looper tension. You may then need to tighten the lower looper tension.

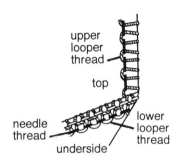

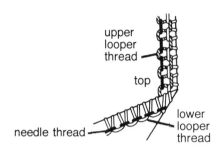

Create a Reversible Edge

There are times when your heavy decorative thread will **only** work in the upper looper. To make the edge look the same on both sides, loosen the upper looper tension until it "wraps" the edge and tighten the lower looper tension until the lower looper thread disappears. With a 2–thread stitch, tighten the needle and loosen the looper.

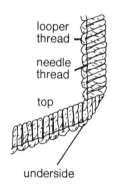

Stitch Length Affects Tension

If you maintain the same stitch width, but change the length, you will need to change the looper tensions as follows:

The **longer** the stitch, the more looper thread you'll need. **Loosen** the looper tensions so more thread flows through.

The **shorter** the stitch length, the less looper thread you'll need. **Tighten** the looper tensions so less thread flows through.

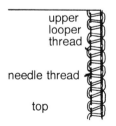

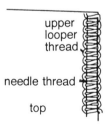

Hiccups (Narrowed Stitches)

Sue came up with the term "hiccups" for the narrowing of a stitch. This is caused by serging too fast, the thread getting caught in a thread guide, or the thread getting caught on the spool and not reeling off freely.

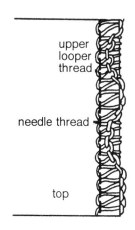

How to Fix Hiccups

1. Rip out stitching to just above the hiccup. You must begin new stitching without a chained tail (see page 33).

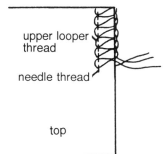

2. Lower needle into the seam line a few stitches above where you stopped ripping as shown.

3. When stitching is completed, go back to the hiccup area and pull all the threads to the wrong side. Knot. Dab knots with a seam sealant like Fray Check, Alene's Stop Fraying or Plaid's No-Fray. Trim or bury threads in seam.

What Happens if You Run Out of Thread?

If you are serging along and run out of thread, oh my! However, you can fix the stitching using the same steps for fixing hiccups. You might need to unravel some stitches to have enough to tie, but you won't need to rip out the entire seam.

CHAPTER 5.

Failsafe Fundamentals, Including Differential Feed

In this chapter we'll show you tips that can make a BIG difference in your serging (and sanity!).

Removing Thread From the Stitch Finger

Frequently you will need to remove the chained tail threads from the stitch finger in order to pull on, release, or separate the threads. Use this technique for:

- Separating threads for tying a less bulky knot (see page 36).

- Separating threads to check threading (see page 22).

- Tying on and rethreading the machine.

- Turning corners.

- Repairing "hiccups."

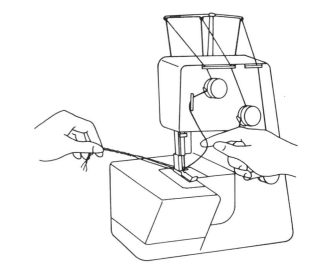

It's easy! Just pull slack in the **needle thread** between the needle and the tension guide as shown. Pull **slightly** for turning corners and a lot for separating threads.

Note: Some new serger models have thread-tension release levers that streamline pulling the threads off the finger into an unchained tail any length desired.

Ripping Stitches—The Easiest Methods

- On a 2–thread overedge, pull on needle and looper threads equally and at the same time. They will pull out easily.

- On a 2–thread chain, pull on the looper thread and it will pull right out.

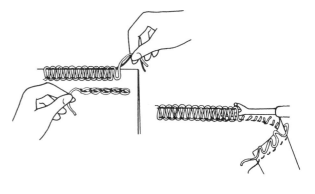

- On 3– and 3/4–thread stitches, slip a small seam ripper under the loops on one side, cutting them. The needle and looper threads on the other side will easily pull out.

- Or, find the needle thread (the shortest thread) and pull on it. It will gather up the fabric and then pull out. Then the looper loops will fall off.

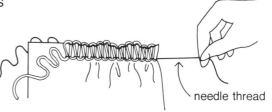

needle thread

Knotting Next to the Fabric

Pati was a 10-year-old 4-H member when she learned this neat trick for knotting next to the fabric. Our workshop students were awed by this simple method.

1. Tie the knot loosely. Slip a straight pin into its center.

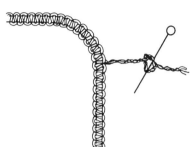

2. Wiggle the knot over the pin until it gets close to the fabric edge.

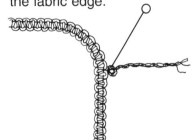

3. With a pin at the fabric edge, slip the knot to the point. Pull tightly.

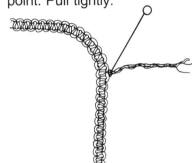

Securing the End of a Seam by Hand

The loose loops at the beginning or end of a seam can ravel out. You can't backstitch on a serger! Use one of the following methods to secure a seam:

- **Tie a knot and put a dab of seam sealant** such as Fray Check, No-Fray, or Stop Fraying on it. After it dries, cut off the excess chain. (Use rubbing alcohol to remove unwanted seam sealant).

  Note: To make the seam sealant more "controllable," use a pin or your finger to dab it onto the knot. Sue puts hers into an empty nail polish bottle and uses the brush to apply it.

- **Bury the chain.**

1. Thread it through a large blunt-pointed tapestry or double-edged needle or a loop turner.

2. Pull the chained tail under tie looper threads and cut off any excess.

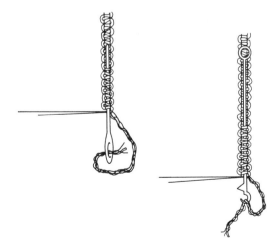

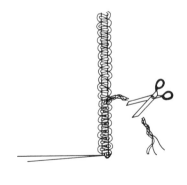

Secure the End of a Seam by Machine

It's easy and if you follow our instructions carefully, you won't get a loop of chained tail threads on the edge of the fabric as shown at the right.

At the beginning of a seam

1. Stitch one stitch into fabric edge.

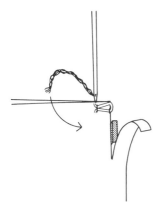

2. **Then** lift the presser foot and bring the chain to the front.

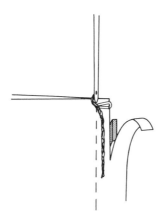

3. Pull on the chain to make it narrow. Place it on the seam allowance and serge over it.

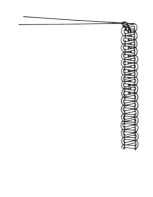

At the end of a seam

1. Serge one stitch off the edge of the fabric. Gently slip the chain off the stitch finger (pulling a slight amount of slack above the needle will this easier—see page 33). Raise the presser foot. Flip the fabric over and to the front of the presser foot.

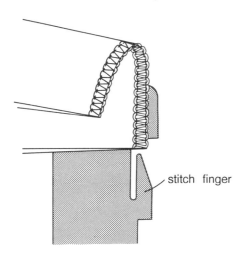

stitch finger

2. Lower the presser foot and stitch 1" to 2" over the last few stitches. Be careful not to cut into the stitches already sewn. Chain off and trim the chain.

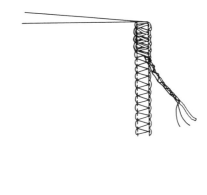

Stitching in a Circle

There are two ways to stitch in a circle. However, entirely avoid serging exposed edges in a circle, use our orders on pages 45.

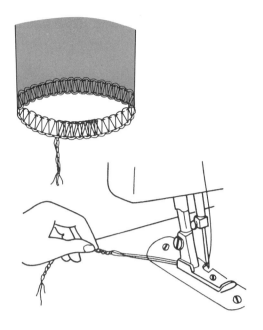

- **Stitch over beginning** stitches 1/2" to 1", then off the edge without cutting previous stitches. Tie a knot near the fabric. Put seam sealant on the knot and cut off the excess chain. This method can look messy unless you are using a thread that covers well; therefore, we generally reserve it for hem edge finishing.

- **Stitches meet without overlapping**. This gives neater results but takes practice!

1. Pull out unchained threads (see page 33). This is important if you want a tiny invisible knot.

2. Always begin serging in the **middle** of a long edge, NOT on a curve. **Always** skim the edges with your knives for even width serging. Stop serging when the knives reach the beginning stitches.

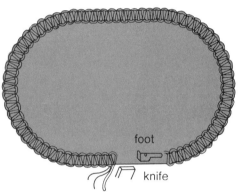

foot

knife

3. Raise the upper knife and continue serging **two** stitches over the beginning stitches. This is difficult if you can't raise the knife on your machine.

4. Again, pull out about 3" to 4" of unchained tail thread.

5. Bring threads to the wrong side and tie knots in the tails. Dab knots with seam sealant, then cut off excess thread or weave the tails into your serging.

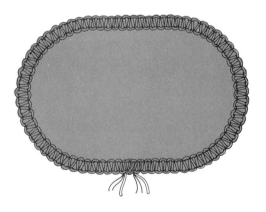

   Alternative: After stitching over 2 or 3 of previous stitches, raise the presser foot, turn the fabric toward the back of the presser foot, and serge off the edge with the presser foot up. The needle "jumps" off the edge without making any more stitches. Tie the tail threads on the wrong side.

   Note: Use this technique if you have a seam allowance to trim away. Cut away a 2" section of the seam allowance where you plan to begin and end your stitching. Then proceed as above, beginning in the middle of the cutaway. Do not make this cut out section on a curve!

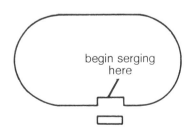

begin serging here

Turning Inside Corners

Inside corners are easier to finish than outside. Use the following technique:

1. Serge until the knife touches the corner. Stop with the needle in the fabric.

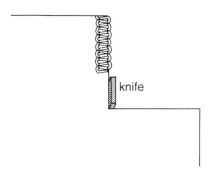

2. Straighten the corner without lifting the presser foot. You will have a "V" fold of fabric. Don't worry, the pleat will disappear after serging.

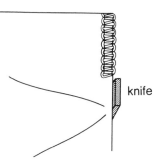

3. Finish serging the straightened edge.

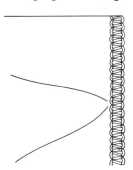

4. Now the inside corner is finished. The stitches will appear slightly rounded rather than a right angle.

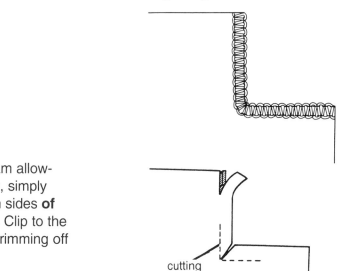

cutting line

Note: If your inside corner has a seam allowance that needs to be trimmed away, simply mark the cutting line within 1" of both sides **of** the corner using a washable marker. Clip to the corner. Serge, as described above, trimming off the seam allowance.

Turning Outside Corners

Pati's mother-in-law learned to sew on a serger by making flannel receiving blankets. She got lots of practice turning corners! Try the following technique:

1. Serge up to the corner and off the edge ONE stitch.

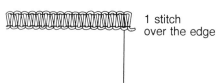

1 stitch over the edge

2. Raise the needle.

3. Pull a small amount of slack in the needle thread—a little finger's worth! This will help you remove the fabric from the stitch finger. Be careful. Too much slack will leave a loop on the corner. Experiment until you determine the right amount of slack required. If you accidentally pull too much, pull on the thread just above the tension dial.

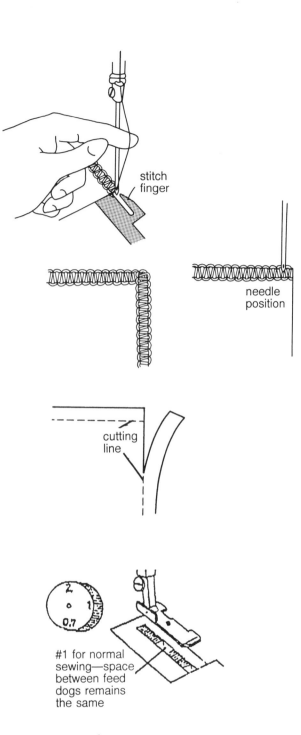

stitch finger

needle position

4. Pivot the fabric. Lower the needle into the fabric **BEFORE** lowering the presser foot, or the needle won't end up where you want it! The needle can be anywhere between the top edge and the seam line. We find we get better coverage of the corner when it is closer to the top edge.

5. Continue sewing the next edge.

Note: If three is a seam allowance, trim it away for **2"** before serging to the corner. Remember, your knife is in front of the needle, so you can't turn a corner without first removing the seam allowance!

cutting line

Differential Feed

Sergers have two sets of feed dogs or teeth that move under the presser foot on the machine. Generally, they move in unison at the same rate of speed. **Differential feed dogs** can move at different rates. The speed of the front feed dog is controlled by a dial or lever with three settings, 0.5 or 0.7, 1, and 2. Some are also variable between settings.

With the dial set on number 1, the feed dogs move at the same rate and the space between them remains the same.

With the differential feed set on number 2, the front feet dog moves twice as much fabric under the presser foot as the rear feed dog lets out, creating a gathering or "easing" effect. The space between the feed dogs appears greater. This prevents stretch and is great for knits.

With differential feed dogs set on numbers 0.5 or 0.7, the front feed dog moves 5/10 or 7/10 as much fabric under the pressure foot as the rear feed dog lets out, creating a "stretching" effect. The space between the feed dogs appears smaller.

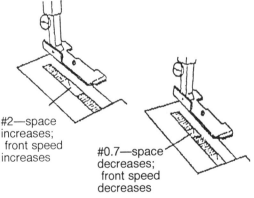

#1 for normal sewing—space between feed dogs remains the same

#2—space increases; front speed increases

#0.7—space decreases; front speed decreases

Where You Can Use Differential Feed

Set above 1, up to 2, the "plus" setting:

- Keeps knits from stretching

Without differential feed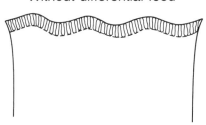

With differential feed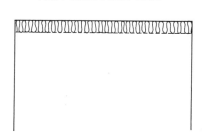

- Gathers lightweight fabrics.

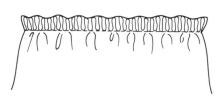

- Eases the lower layer onto the top layer. Place the layer you are easing next to the feed dogs.

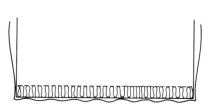

- Prevents stretch when finishing the edge of a circle so it won't become wavy.

Set below 1, usually 0.5 or 0.7, the "minus" setting:

- Prevents puckers in silkies.

- Prevents puckers when sewing a rolled edge on lightweight fabrics.

- Prevents puckers when roll-edging the crossgrain on ruffles, napkins, hems, etc.

CHAPTER 6.
Stabilizing Decorative Serging

Serging is more durable and the stitch width more consistent, when the edge or seam is stabilized. Without stabilizing, some exposed seams and edges, particularly on knits, can stretch out and ripple when serged, worn, or laundered. Gail noticed this on several of her daughter's single-layer tee-shirts; the serged necklines soon stretched or popped out. The Palmer/Pletsch Sewing Vacation students have also realized better results with stabilizing—more uniform stitches and less stretching.

Stabilizing isn't always necessary. If in doubt, test on scraps of your fabric cut on the same grain as your project.

Stabilizing Decorate (Exposed) Seams

Before deciding whether a seam or edge needs stabilizing, consider the serging stitch. The 4/2–thread and 5–thread stitches are the most stable (see page 11), and the stretchiest are the 3/4– and 3–thread overlock. Generally, the wider the stitch, the more stable the seam.

Note: A close satin stitch can cause stretching of a seam or edge, due to thread density. To stabilize shoulder, neckline, front **seams**, or seams in any problem area, try one of the following:

Sew seam with a row of conventional, straight stitching first, then serge seam allowances together. Or, add the straight row after serging.

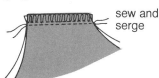

sew and serge

Serge using a 4/2–thread or 5–thread seam.

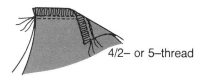

4/2– or 5–thread

Serge over a self-fabric selvage strip placed on the wrong side of the fabric. The color and texture will match your garment.

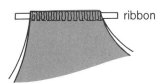

ribbon

Serge over braid, ribbon, yarn, topstitching thread, or pearl cotton.

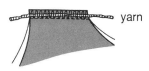

yarn

Flatlock over 1/8" braid or ribbon.

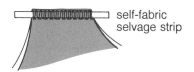

self-fabric selvage strip

Note: For additional stability, press serged seams to one side and edgestitch to garment to secure.

Stabilizing Decorative (Exposed) Edges

There are several ways to stabilize stretch-prone edges:

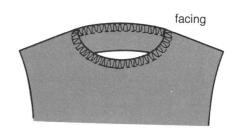

facing

- **Facings**—Cut facings from self- or contrast fabric. Wrong sides together, serge to garment. After serging, leave the facing full width or trim to 1/2"–1". Interface facing with a lightweight fusible for extra body.

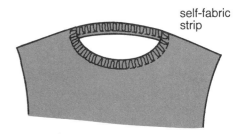

self-fabric strip

- **Narrow self-fabric strips**—Serge 3/4"–1" strips of self-fabric to garment edges, wrong sides together. Trim excess to serging. Use lengthwise grain for stability and bias when give is desired.

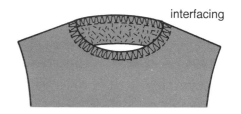

interfacing

- **Fusible**—3/4"–1" wide strips of fusible tricot such as Stacy's Easy Knit or similar fusible tricots; they are great for adding **both** body **and** stability to an edge or to back an entire piece.

yarn

- **Yarn, pearl cotton, buttonhole twist, or elastic cord**—Serge over any of these. Tails can be drawn up, easing to fit. Secure tails with a knot and weave under loops on wrong side. This technique stabilizes, but doesn't add body. We prefer it when the silhouette demands softness like an angora sweater, or the fabric is stable like boiled wool.

  A special foot such as a tape sewing or cording foot makes this easier (see pages 34). Otherwise practice feeding the cord through the hole of your regular foot, laying it just to the left of the knife. This is easier than placing it under the foot.

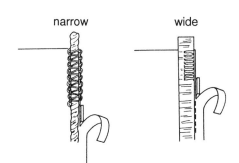

- **Ribbons**—Use ribbons only on straight or slightly curved edges. Place ribbon on the wrong side of fabric and serge with ribbon on top. Avoid cutting the ribbon. Serge **over** narrow 1/8"–1/4" ribbon and **through** wider ones.

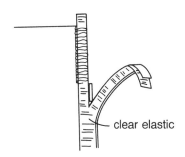

- **Clear elastic**—3/8" clear elastic works well on knits. You can serge through it and even trim it even with the fabric edge without destroying the elastic stretch.

CHAPTER 7.

In Only Five Steps: Decoratively Serged Tops and Jackets

Flat construction is perfect for single layer and reversible clothes. It eliminates serging in a circle. Start with casual tops, then serge ahead to jackets and coats!

Sleeveless, Round Neckline, Pullover Tops and Dresses

Use single layer (or double for reversible looks) of interlock, doubleknit, singleknit, or lightweight woven fabric and the following sewing order.

Be sure to stabilize exposed edges if necessary. Serge fabric right or wrong side together as follows:

1. Serge one shoulder seam.

2. Serge to finish the neckline.

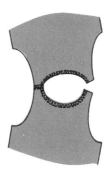

3. Serge the other shoulder seam. Then finish armhole edges.

4. Serge one underarm seam and serge finish hem edge.

5. Serge the other underarm seam. Tie and bury any chain tail threads. If desired, topstitch exposed **seams** flat.

"V"-Neckline Pullover Tops

Add a center front seam to make continuous decorative serging easy on "V"-neck tops. Serge fabric right or wrong sides together as follows:

1. Serge both shoulder seams.

2. Serge finish the neckline.

3. Serge the center front seam right or wrong sides together, whichever you prefer. If you serge the neckline and front in the direction of the arrows, serging can be continuous.

4. Serge armhole seams. Then stitch one underarm seam and serge finish the hem

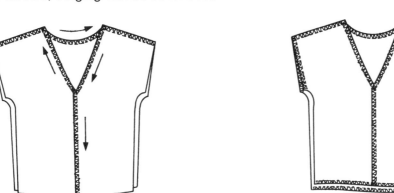

5. Now serge the other underarm seam. Tie and bury any chain tail threads. If desired, topstitch exposed seams flat.

Single Layer Jackets and Coats

Who would have ever thought a jacket or coat could be as simple to sew as a blouse? Look for stable meltons, double-knit, double-faced, or boiled wool, sweaterknit, or even upholstery fabric. Two medium-weight fabrics in contrasting colors can be used wrong sides together to simulate the look of double-faced fabrics. Use a balanced stitch and the same thread in both loopers or wrap the edge (see page 30), to make the edge reversible.

Gail's Five-Step Jacket (or Coat)

Gail made this jacket from a very heavy wool melton that is inherently ravel-resistant, making the single layer garment very durable and easy to sew.

Note: Gail has used this serging order for blouses, too, finishing with a narrow, rolled edge.

1. Decoratively serge finish the outer edges of the upper collar. Serge the shoulders and one underarm seam right sides together.

2. Starting at the lower edge of the open side seam, decoratively serge the hem, front edge, collar to neckline, other front and the rest of the hem.

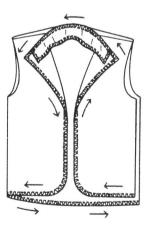

3. Sew the open side seam.

4. Decoratively serge finish the sleeve hem. Seam and set in sleeves.

5. Sew button and buttonholes. VOILA!...a finished jacket!

Marta's Lapped Variation

Palmer/Pletsch's resident speed sewing and serger expert, Marta Alto, has devised another single layer sewing order for coats and jackets. For jackets made out of woolens, she prefers not to have serged side, shoulder, and center back seams. She prefers to finish one layer and lap and topstitch them.

1. Decoratively serge finish all edges of collar.

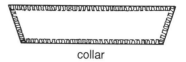

collar

2. Serge front side and shoulders and left center back seams. Lap front over back at sides and left back over right and topstitch. Stop sewing center back 4" from bottom.

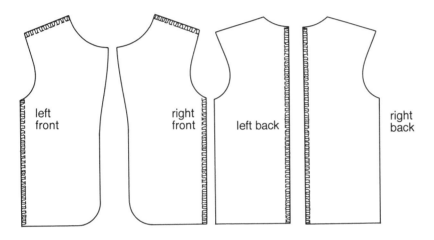

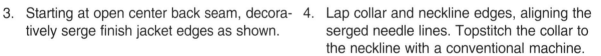

left front   right front   left back   right back

3. Starting at open center back seam, decoratively serge finish jacket edges as shown.

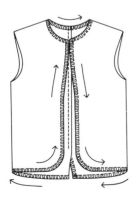

4. Lap collar and neckline edges, aligning the serged needle lines. Topstitch the collar to the neckline with a conventional machine.

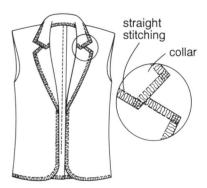

straight stitching

collar

Coordinate Other Design Details

We generally reserve dramatic **contrasting** decorative stitching for lapels, collars, and hemlines. However, when the color matches or is a subtle contrast, other design details can also be tastefully and decoratively serged, such as the following:

- Belt edges and patch pockets

- Sleeve seams and edges

- Yokes

- Couched serger braid

- Applique edges

- Other embellishments and accents, such as the "squiggles" shown here (see pages 73–75).

Serger Pro Showcase

When we were discussing the revision of this book, Pati came up with the wonderful idea of featuring garments made by the industry's top serging professionals. Through our travel, teaching, and writing, we three authors have come in contact with incredibly creative designers and skillful technicians. We are sharing here their inspiring serged projects and the methods used to make them.

From left to right: *Lynn Raasch, Terri Burns, Pati Palmer* and (front) *Marta Alto model their own creations, each featuring a myriad of decorative-serging techniques.* **Created by:** *Paula Marineau, Pati Palmer, Marla Kazell, Lynn Raasch, Marta Alto, and Terri Burns.* **Submitted by:** *Pati Palmer, Palmer/Pletsch Associates.* **Serger brands:** *assorted.*

Wearable Serged Art (overleaf)

We call these wearable-art items "Jackets by Committee." It all started when Pati needed a jacket to wear while moderating an art quilt fashion show in Paducah, Kentucky. Pati and her colleagues consulted and brainstormed a basic idea that combined decorative serging with a method of quilting used by Portland designer Paula Marineau.

Pati's jacket

Pati had Springs Industries' new 60"-wide linen in a green shade, from which the color scheme evolved (p. 51, far right). She bought one-yard lengths of raw silk in magenta, blue, green, and red. She cut the fabrics into 6"–8" strips, then along the edges with a variety of decorative stitches using decorative threads. Some pieces were roll-edged; some edged with a wide balanced stitch; and some were flatlocked down the center of the strip from the wrong side so a ladder appeared on the right side.

Pati chose an oversized cardigan jacket pattern. She gave the pattern and serged jacket strips, as well as the linen, to Portland artist Paula Marineau. Paula cut the pattern from cotton flannel. Then she laid the strips on the flannel base, lapping serged edges over the raw edges of the next strip. Strips were secured by edge stitching. Raw edges on the short ends of strips were hidden in seams or by strips turned perpendicularly.

Piping was used between some of the strips. Where there was an exposed raw edge, Paula added narrow bias strips. She made them with the Clover Bias Tape Maker in order to have even-width bias with the edges turned under. These strips were edge stitched in place. Decorative machine stitching was added to the center of some of the bias strips.

Marla Kazell then constructed the jacket, piping its edges and sleeve hems. She lined the jacket with cotton chintz and, in the upper back area, stitched a 6"-wide strip of decorated fabrics echoing the outside of the jacket. This elegant touch is a Paula Marineau trademark, seen only when the jacket is removed.

Marta's jacket

Marta Alto saw the unused stack of decorated strips; she chose the reds, adding purple to match an existing skirt (p. 51, center front). She also selected a shorter jacket pattern with princess seaming. She created serger piping for the cardigan's edges by serging over yarn and Seams Great. Even though she started with many of the same strips, her jacket looks different because of the way she placed the strips and combined the colors. Marta lined her jacket with silk; the flannel base was heavy, so she didn't need interfacing.

Lynn's jacket

The bag of strips (now shorter and narrower) went to Lynn Raasch next. Lynn added more blues and purples (p. 51, far left). She chose the same pattern as Marta because the small garment sections worked well with the smaller strips. Lynn emphasized the silhouette of the jacket in her piecing design, so the final effect has a more pronounced stripe than the others. Lynn faced the jacket with a lighter weight fabric, which she interfaced and then lined.

Terri's jacket

Terri Burns did not inherit the bag of strips, but she was in on the original idea. She, too, went shopping for silk yardage, planning to make blue her dominant color (p. 51, rear center). Independently of Pati, she picked the same color range—blues, purples, magentas, greens. In addition to the silks, Terri inserted some Ultrasuede strips on which she serged a blanket stitch. With Decor 6 in the needle, which was taken out of the tension dial, and Woolly Nylon in the loopers, which were tightened, she serged slowly along the edge, creating a blanket-stitch look. Terri's jacket was lined, faced and interfaced.

How-to hints

• Remember that the ladder side of flatlocking is the needle thread (shown on Pati's jacket); choose the needle-thread type and color accordingly.

• Save time and fabric by utilizing Seams Great when making serged piping.

Related page references: For decorative-thread options, see pages 13–19; for serged piping, see page 99; for blanket stitch, see page 97.

Instant Classic (opposite)

Basic black and flashy flounces

Black is the perfect foil for flashy color. The dress is black taffeta with a chiffon overskirt and four layers of net ruffles. Betty Quinell serges the edges of four net ruffles on the underskirt with colored metallic threads. She uses a balanced 3-thread stitch, with Candlelight by YLI in both loopers, and serges over 25# test fishing line and black knitting yarn. The cording foot facilitates smooth feeding of the line and yarn under the stitch.

Betty suggests that you leave a lot of thread chain at both ends, because the fishing line tends to pull up and want to slip out of the serging. When you're finished serging the ruffle, stretch and smooth it out slowly. Then glue to secure the ends of the fishing line to the net.

She repeats the metallic motif at the shoulder ruffles and on the edges of the rose at the waistband. The rose is constructed of leftover taffeta and net, with black ribbon and a black button center. She uses a rolled edge on the hem of the chiffon.

How-to hints

• Gently stretch netting or tulle over the fishing line. Too-rigorous stretching can tear these relatively delicate fabrics, especially tulle.

• To completely cover the fishing line, and yield the most flouncing, adjust for a short stitch.

• When serge-finishing yards and yards of ruffles, start with the largest spool or cone available in the looper(s) positions. (YLI now sells 500-yard cones of Candlelight. Also look for large, often discount-priced, cones of metallic needlepunch yarn, which usually feeds glitch-free through serger guides.)

Related page references: for metallic threads, see page 16; for fishing-line flounces, see page 97; for rolled edges, see pages 93–101; for special serger feet, see page 146.

To set off the stunning black silhouette, multicolored metallic-edged flounces are flared with fishing-line and yarn filler cords. ***Created by:*** *Betty Quinell.* ***Submitted by:*** *Juki of America.* ***Serger brand:*** *Juki.*

Elegant Serged Embellishments (opposite)

Appliquéd jacket

Serger techniques and linen go together like peaches and ice cream. Here serger appliqué is featured on a suit by Tammy Dunrud (p.55, far right). Appliqué shapes were cut and edged with a balanced 3-thread stitch, using Woolly Nylon. The corner thread tails were treated with seam sealant; when dry, they were cut off. The shapes were then appliquéd to the garment, using a straight stitch on the sewing machine.

This jacket contains a multitude of serger techniques: a decorative chain stitch on the sleeves, serger piping on the back yoke, serged ribbon tucks, and 3-thread flatlock.

Giraffe-appliqué T-shirt

People look twice when they see this gray-green T-shirt coming (p. 55, far left). A gentle serged giraffe nibbles leaves. The leaves are outlined with a balanced 3-thread stitch, then appliquéd with a straight stitch. Agnes Mercik combines two threads in the upper looper, a Madeira metallic with a YLI Woolly Nylon. This gives a shine to the edge, yet the coverage is better filled in by the woolly nylon.

The mane is an organdy ruffle, made with a cording foot and a rolled hem over fishing line. The giraffe is outlined with serger piping. The heavier inner lines are created by serging heavy thread over sport-weight knitting yarn and then couching it to the giraffe with a sewing machine, using the braiding foot and a zigzag. Details of the face are stitched with decorative sewing-machine stitches.

Couched jacket

You see this type of undulating couching everywhere in ready-to-wear (below left). Agnes Mercik first fuses tricot interfacing to linen yardage. This not only makes the garment less wrinkle-prone, but also supports the embroidery. Agnes first draws her design on tearaway, loads Decor 6 into the bobbin of her sewing machine, and stitches the design, underside up. This lays the Decor 6 on the surface of the jacket.

Agnes serged a long chain of Decor 6 in both loopers over thick knitting yarn. Then she used the leather roller foot on her sewing machine to couch the serger trim next to the decorative line she had already stitched, giving a subtle shadow effect. Agnes chose that foot because it enables her to really see what she is doing and to maneuver tight edges. She uses a variegated copper thread and couches with a pin stitch, since she feels a zigzag would be too heavy for the serger trim.

Couched T-shirt

This black long-sleeved T-shirt has a striking Native American motif (p. 55, rear center). Agnes made the hair with serger trim in lots of combinations of silver threads and variegated metallics. The decorations are worked on flat fabric; then the pattern is cut out. The serger trim is couched to the bodice front, expanded by flowing rows of straight stitch. The feathers are a metallic fabric backed with interfacing, edged with a balanced 3-thread stitch, and then appliquéd with tearaway underneath to prevent tunneling. Decorative stitches embellish the feathers, and beads and silver are hand-stitched for earrings. Even with all this three-dimensional work, the garment can be hand-washed or put on a gentle cycle in the washing machine.

How-to Hints

• For the easiest, fastest serge-finished appliqué, stick with simple, geometric shapes.

• When chainstitching decoratively, use decorative thread in the chainstitch looper, and place the project right-side-down on the serger.

• Custom blend your own threads, combining textures, weights and colors in one looper, as Agnes did on the giraffe-appliqué edge. Place extra spools or cones on coned thread stands or in bowls or jars behind the serger.

• When making 3-thread serger trim, try using melt-adhesive thread, such as Thread-Fuse or Stitch 'N'

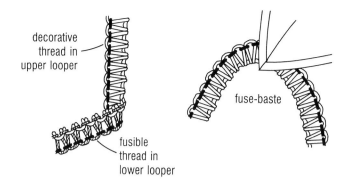

decorative thread in upper looper

fuse-baste

fusible thread in lower looper

Fuse in the lower looper of a balanced-tension stitch. Then, the trim can be fuse-basted to the project to prevent slippage and eliminate pinning when couching. Adjust the looper tensions to prevent the fusible thread from showing on the right side.

Related page references: For decorative-thread options, see pages 13–19; for serger piping, see page 99; for fishing line ruffles, see page 75; for chainstitching, see pages 106, 120.

Elegant serged embellishments include serged appliqué, fishing-line ruffles, and couching, plus intriguing stitches and threads.
Created by: (right) *Tammy Dunrud;* (all others) *Agnes Mercik.* **Submitted by:** *JoAnn Pugh, Bernina of America.*
Serger brand: *Bernina.*

Pretty and Practical Serging

Ruffled ribbing T-shirt

Lettuce-edged ribbing gives a cheerful texture to this red, white, and blue sweatshirt made by Linnette Whicker of Arlington, Texas (p. 57, left). Use differential feed on a setting less than 1 to stretch the edge of the ribbing. If you don't have differential feed, use your hands to stretch the ribbing in front of the presser foot. Linnette uses two strands of Woolly Nylon in the upper looper and all-purpose thread in the needle and lower looper, to roll the edge.

Linnette cuts out a T-shirt pattern (but not the neckline) from a blue interlock. She marks a tick-tack-toe pattern on the bodice, making 6" squares. Stitching the ribbing in long strips, she then cuts them to fit alternate squares. The top edge of the ribbing is stitched in 1/2" overlapping rows to the foundation fabric, starting with the bottom row. Linnette fuses ribbon on top of the tick-tack-toe lines, then topstitches along each edge. Finally, the neckline is cut, the garment is serged together, and ribbing is added to the neckline, cuffs, and hem. The cuffs and hem ribbing are also lettuce-edged.

Ribbon-trimmed shell

A good way to practice your skills is to use new-to-you techniques and materials on simple clothing, like this rayon shell (p. 57, center). Using Decor 6 in the upper looper and all-purpose thread in the needle and lower looper, three lines of horizontal 3-thread flatlocking are serged above the bust, crossing two vertical lines. Linnette press-marked the lines first, as stitching guides. She likes using the blind-hem foot to help guide the fabric through without cutting it.

Serging-sampler dress

This charming girl's knit dress (p. 57, right) uses gathered strips of the skirt material inserted into the center of the sleeve. Kathy Wilkinson of Mt. Prospect, Illinois, elongates a basic T-shirt pattern, adding a woven fabric skirt to a band at the base of the bodice. The skirt is ruffled onto the band with a serger shirring foot. At the top of the band, Kathy uses a serger piping foot to insert piping between the band and the bodice. She splits the sleeve into three pieces, inserting ruffling at each edge in one step with the shirring foot. When the pieces are serged together, each seam has two ruffles in it.

At the hem, Kathy uses the ribbon foot, flatlocking over 1/4" ribbon. She applies plastic beads in a diagonal line on the front, using the beading foot. The embellished garment is still machine-washable.

How-to hints

• Flatlock bead strands effortlessly, using a special beading or pearl/sequin foot. The beads on the strand should be no larger than 4mm; several sizes and types are readily available in most fabric and craft stores (including Cross-locked Glass Beads, now distributed by E-Z International.)

• Adjust your serger for the widest, longest flatlock stitch. Place the strand over the front of the foot, and under the back of the foot, in the channels; the strand will be safely positioned to the right of the needle and to the left of the knives. Start with the bead-strand tail a few inches long, so you can hold it while serging, to advance the stitch. Serge over the bead strand, right side of the project on top. The beads will peek out of the upper looper.

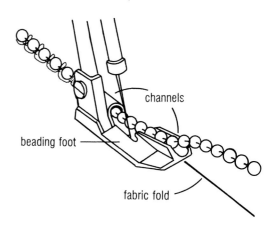

channels

beading foot

fabric fold

• If heavy thread is used in the upper looper, the look is similar to crocheted beading. (The heavier the thread, the more the beads will be covered.)

• If you don't have a special beading foot, and you are using a fine strand, place it under the back of the foot and over the front, between the needle and the knives. To avoid accidental cutting of the strand, butt it against the front-foot ledge. Hold the bead strand taut as it passes under the foot to prevent puckering. If using larger diameter beads that won't feed smoothly under the foot, remove the foot, guiding the strand through manually. Also try serging with the presser foot up, and down, to see which produces the best results.

Related page references: for ribbing, see pages 111–116; for serged sweatshirts or tops, see pages 111–121; for flatlocking, see pages 83–91; for more bead applications, see pages 61–62, 106; specialty serger feet, see pages 146–148.

Decorative serging customizes casual clothes; techniques include lettuce-edged ribbing, flatlocked ribbon and flatlocked beading. **Created by:** *Linnette Whicker* (left and center) *and Kathy Wilkinson* (right). **Submitted by:** *Louise Gerigk, Pfaff American Sales.* **Serger brand:** *Pfaff Hobbylock.*

Speedy Serged Sophisticates (overleaf)

Decoratively serge-finished coat

Cindy Cummins's successful serger pattern comes complete with step-by-step instructions on how to make this attractive, speedy "Coat in a Day." In addition to edging it with a wide, balanced 3-thread stitch, Cindy has added coordinating chainstitch passementerie on the yoke area.

For the 3-thread serged edge, Cindy recommends using Woolly Nylon, Pearl Crown Rayon, Ribbon Floss, Decor 6, Success yarn, or needlepunch yarn in both the upper and lower loopers, with all-purpose thread in the needle. Practice on scraps of the fashion fabric, fine-tuning the tension. The serged shoulder/sleeve seam is exposed, so she first stitches this seam on the conventional sewing machine to prevent slipping.

For the passementerie, Cindy puts decorative thread in the upper looper and all-purpose thread in the lower looper and needle. She loosens the upper looper tension so that the decorative thread spreads to the full stitch width, forming continuous "S" shapes. Cindy

Sophisticated "Coat in a Day" and "Dress in an Hour" patterns incorporate balanced-tension edge finishing and matching passe-menterie braid, also created with the serger. **Created and submitted by**: *Cindy Cummins, The Cutting Edge.* **Serger brand**: *baby lock.*

chains off about three to four yards of passementerie chain and pulls to smooth the chain. To set, relax and straighten the decorative chain, she wraps it around a cone of thread. If possible, she leaves the chain on the cone overnight, or at least two hours. She applies the passementerie to the coat by zigzagging it in place, careful that the zigzag width is not wider than the passementerie; the zigzag stitches should burrow in the trim.

Serger appliquéd dress

Cindy's newest pattern is "Dress in an Hour," from which this serger appliquéd dress was made. The appliqués are first backed with paper-backed fusible web; the paper is removed before serging the edges. Use a balanced 3-thread stitch on all edges with decorative thread in the upper looper; fusible, melt-adhesive thread in the lower looper; and conventional coned thread in the needle. Do not use seam sealant on the corners, because it will interfere with fusing. Instead, bury the tails underneath the appliqués.

Cindy creates passementerie and applies it to the dress with a sewing machine. Then she fuses the appliqués in place over the passementerie, using a Teflon press cloth. The melt-adhesive fusible thread secures the serged appliqué edges; add durability by edgestitching with decorative or straight sewing-machine stitches.

How-to hints

• To ensure reversibility of the 3-thread stitch, especially important along jacket or coat roll lines, use the same decorative thread in the upper and lower loopers.

• When using a 2-thread overedge to finish reversible edges, decorative thread is recommended for the nee-

dle, too. Some types that will pass through the needle eye and the fabric smoothly include topstitching or buttonhole twist thread, Success yarn, needlepunch yarn, or YLI's Jeanstitch.

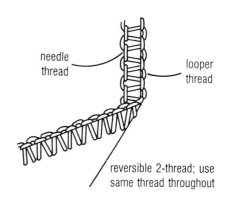

needle thread · looper thread · reversible 2-thread; use same thread throughout

• Position, then fuse-baste melt-adhesive thread, using a dry iron on the right side. Then, again from the right side, steam in place to permanently secure. (Exposing melt-adhesive thread to steam—before it is positioned—can shrink the thread and collapse the serged edge.)

• Using your pattern guidesheet, plot decorative serging order to facilitate continuous stitching, minimize rethreading and decrease the number of turned corners.

Related page references: for decorative-thread options, see pages 13–19; for decorative-serging basics, see pages 21–31; for decorative-serging orders, see pages 45–49.

Quick Conversion Sweatshirt

Conversion sweatshirt

Bring casual elegance to any sweatshirt by fashioning removable epaulets of glitzy fabric. Sue Hausmann of Viking says her "Conversion Sweatshirts" are like a conversion van: "You add stuff to them which makes them worth lots more money and lots more fun!"

Begin with an oversized man's sweatshirt. Cut off the lower edge ribbing and cut up the center front. Stabilize the ribbing with fusible tricot interfacing, divide it into two pieces, and seam to finish one short end on each piece, wrong sides together. Then serge seam one ribbing piece to each side of the center front, placing the

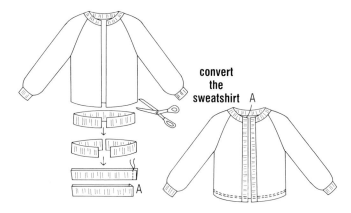

convert
the
sweatshirt   A

A

Transformed from an oversized man's sweatshirt, accented with removable serged epaulets and streaming with decorative threads. **Created and submitted by:** *Sue Hausmann, Viking Sewing Machine Company.* **Serger brand:** *Viking Huskylock.*

seamed short ends at the neckline edges. Here the ribbing is turned to the inside and topstitched in place, but for a cardigan, the ribbing could be left outside. Turn up the hem and blindstitch or topstitch with twin needles.

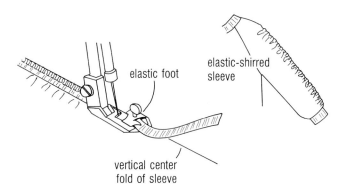

elastic foot

elastic-shirred sleeve

vertical center fold of sleeve

On the inside of the sleeves, serge 1/4" elastic to the vertical center, from the shoulder cap to the wrist, using an elastic foot. This shirrs the sleeve, adding contouring.

Removable epaulets. Gather a collection of glitzy fabrics like lamés, metallics, etc. Approximately 1/4 yard of six different fabrics is plenty. Cut the fabric into 9" x 11"

pieces. Set up your machine for a narrow rolled edge, with metallic thread in the upper looper. Serge along all 9" edges. Then serge parallel to the 11" edge, cutting 3/4"-wide strips, leaving 4"–5" thread chains at each end.

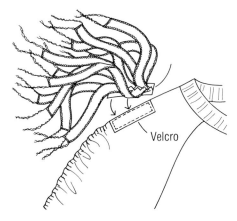

Velcro

Cut two 2-3/4" strips of Velcro, one for each epaulet. On the back of each hook half of the Velcro, pile serged strips and attach them by sewing down the center with a multi-step zigzag stitch. Try on the sweatshirt and mark where your shoulder seam falls. Attach the other half of the Velcro to the outside of the shoulder on the marked seam; straight stitch around the outside of the Velcro strip.

Change the look of your sweatshirt by varying the colors and fabrics used in the epaulets. For more ideas, watch Sue in her public broadcast series, "The Art of Sewing with Sue Hausmann" or refer to her book, *Quick Gifts to Make*, available at Viking dealers.

How to hints

• Test-serge, using metallic threads in the upper looper. Generally, due to the brittleness of the fiber, a looser looper tension is required.

• For the smoothest, pokey-free edge finish, cut the longer side of the epaulet strips parallel with the lengthwise grain. (The lengthwise grain edges finish much more pucker- and ravel-free than crosswise grain edges.)

Related page references: for decorative-thread options, see pages 13–19; for rolled-edges, see pages 93–101; for creative sweatshirts, see pages 111–121.

Serged Silks and Pearls (overleaf)

Silk Jacket

Lace appliqué and a pearl edging raise this pure silk jacket into star status. Mary Sromek of North Royalton, Ohio, starts by cutting the front and back neck facings from fusible tricot, and fusing them to the underside of the front and back. She also fuses a bias band of fusible tricot around the underside of the bottom edge. This gives it a crisp hem without the tendency to pucker. She then cuts a lining from the jacket pattern.

She places monofilament nylon in the right needle and both loopers and sets up for a balanced 3-thread stitch, about 2.5–3.5mm long. Placing the lining and the

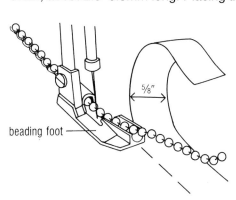

jacket wrong sides together, Mary applies a 3mm pearl strand to the opening edges, using the Huskylock beading foot. She trims off the 5/8" seam allowance.

beading foot

5/8"

The stitch slips between the pearls, the monofilament seems to disappear, and the pearls cover the raw edge.

To join the pearls, Mary serges near the beginning, cuts the pearls to fit the needed length, nudges the beginning and ending together, and serges a bit beyond the beginning. Then she works the threads off the stitch finger, ties them off, and secures them with seam sealant.

The appliqué is a purchased flat bridal lace, to which Mary added hand-stitched beads. She then hand-applied it to the jacket. "I am so busy teaching," says Mary, "and don't have a lot of time for personal sewing. The serger makes everything so fast, I don't mind the extra time for creative hand work."

The silky skirt is quickly constructed by using sew-through elastic at the waistline, serging the side seams, and serging, turning, and topstitching the hem.

How-to hints

• To prevent puckers when applying beads, adjust for "minus" (.5–.7) differential feed setting. Or, without differential feeding, hold the fabric taut, with one hand in front of the foot and one hand behind it.

• Before monofilament-nylon thread slumps off the spool or cone into a tangled mess, cover with thread nets.

• To facilitate smooth, even application of bead strands, try using a beading or pearl/sequin foot. There are now both brand-name and generic types to fit a wide range of sergers.

• Choose the stitch option for beading application that works best for your project. (Mary chose a balanced-tension stitch.) For beads applied to the interior of a pro-

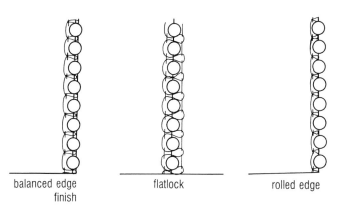

balanced edge finish   flatlock   rolled edge

ject, use a flatlock stitch. For a narrow, reversible beading, use a rolled edge. Start with a stitch width at least as wide as the bead diameter, and a long enough stitch length to expose the individual beads.

Mary Sromek serged pearl beading to her lovely lace-appliquéd jacket and hand-applied individual pearls to the lace. **Created and submitted by:** *Mary Sromek, The Sewing Gallery, North Olmstead, Ohio.* **Serger brand:** *Viking Huskylock.*

• Check the bead care instructions, or test wash or dry clean first, before applying.

• When serging pucker-prone lightweight silkies, adjust for a slightly shorter and narrower than normal stitch and a "minus" .5 or .7 differential feed setting. Also, for these run-sensitive fabrics, it's wise to start with a new needle, in the smallest size recommended for your serger. Keep your thread selections lightweight, too, with specialty serger thread, rayons and Woolly Nylon. Another perfect stitch–fabric match: silkies and delicate 2-thread finishing.

Related page references: for stabilizing edges, see pages 41–42; for flatlocked bead applications, see pages 61–62; for troubleshooting, see page 145.

Color-Blocked Blouses (below)

Budgetwise remnants were flatlocked into larger pieces of fabric, from which blouse patterns were cut. **Created by:** *Betty Quinell, Juki of America.* **Submitted by:** *Juki of America Education Department.* **Serger brand:** *Juki.*

Blouses

Exterior serging lends stylish grace to two color-blocked blouses by Betty Quinell. Betty's favorite part of a fabric store is the remnant table. She loves to flatlock remnants together. Both blouses are constructed in a similar way.

Using metallic YLI Candlelight in the upper looper and all-purpose thread in the needle and lower looper, she flatlocks her remnants together. Because these are polyester-cotton blends and because she widens the stitch bite, she does not have a problem with fraying.

Next Betty lays the pattern pieces over the new yardage and cuts. She flatlocks the sleeve, then flatlocks the sleeve/side seam all at once. Sometimes she uses more durable all-purpose thread for this long seam,

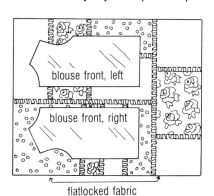

so that the thread will not abrade against itself at the underarm.

For making pockets, she uses a balanced 3-thread stitch and serges all the way around without stopping. On corners, she serges "one stitch shy of the edge," loosens the needle thread above the needle, gently pulls the pocket off the stitch finger, pivots, hand lowers the needle, and begins serging again (see our instructions on page 57). She stops serging when she meets the beginning, removes the pocket from the serger, separates the thread chain into three threads, and uses a large-eyed needle to thread the ends under the stitching. "You cannot tell where I started or stopped," Betty says. Finally, Betty stitches the pocket to the garment with a sewing machine.

Betty constructs collars on the sewing machine, enclosing the raw edges. Then she stitches a balanced 3-thread stitch around the edge, without cutting.

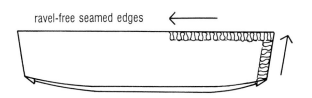

ravel-free seamed edges

Otherwise, the edges might fray. Betty says these garments have been dry-cleaned over and over, with no problem.

How-to hints

• Cut-free flatlocking, when the loops are allowed to hang over the edge slightly, will pull flatter than if you trim. When both layers of fabric are the full width of the

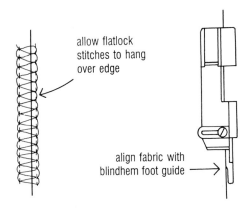

allow flatlock stitches to hang over edge

align fabric with blindhem foot guide →

stitch, there isn't enough room under the flatlock for the stitch to lie flat. Some enthusiasts find that flatlocking with a blindhem foot helps to flatlock without trimming.

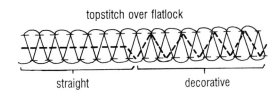

topstitch over flatlock

straight   decorative

• For extra durability, and an interesting grouping of threads, try topstitching (straight or decorative) through the flatlock with invisible nylon thread, matching, or contrasting thread.

• Add dimension, color and texture by flatlocking over decorative thread, cording, narrow ribbon, or beading.

• Create interesting effects by weaving yarn or narrow ribbon in and out of exposed flatlocked ladders.

• Position flatlocking where it won't be continually rubbed or snagged, especially when the looper thread is exposed. Because the stitch floats on the fabric surface, it is vulnerable to surface abrasion.

Related page references: for decorative-thread options, see pages 13–19; for flatlocking, see pages 83–91; for turning corners, see page 37.

Serging Takes Flight! (opposite)

Appliquéd jumpsuit

This easy kite appliqué brings instant color to a child's jumpsuit. Start with a purchased knit garment and use Singer's instructions to make a jumpsuit romper, a clever conversion from an adult sweatshirt or T-shirt. (The sleeves are trimmed off and resewn on to form the romper legs.)

First assemble and decorate the parts of the appliqués. The kites are of primary-colored rip-stop nylon. Edge them with a balanced 3-thread stitch, using Decor 6 in the upper looper. Tuck the tails under the appliqué before stitching it down.

Then work the two kite tails by serging thread chains over three strands of Decor 6, with Decor 6 also in the upper looper. For the kite bows, cut 1" x 1-1/2" ripstop rectangles and edge them with the same 3-thread stitch.

Position the kite tails on the garment and hold them in place with fabric glue.

Topstitch on either side of the chain (or use a double needle) to apply the tails to the garment. Position the appliqués over the kite tails and straight stitch them to the garment along the edge of the serging. Gather the bows by hand in the middle and hand-tack them to the base of the kites as shown.

How-to hint

• Group all decoratively serged elements to minimize time-consuming thread changes.

Related page references: for decorative-thread options, see pages 13–19; for decorative-serging basics, see pages 21–31; for creative sweatshirts, see pages 111–121.

Opposite: This one-piece romper features easy-to-serge-finish kite appliqués, with matching serger-braid tails. **Created and submitted by:** *Singer Educational Department.* **Serger brand:** *Singer Quantumlock.*

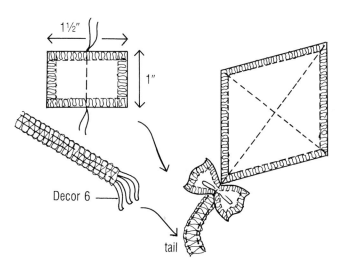

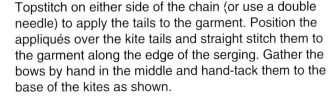

1½"

1"

Decor 6 —

tail

Color-Blocking without Seams (opposite)

Color-blocked jacket

Get the color blocking effect without cutting up a pattern and adding seam allowances. Here Agnes Mercik appliqués linen on linen and fools the eye.

Choose a base color for every garment piece—each can be a different color—and assemble complementary threads and fabrics. In planning your garment, make certain that decorated areas do not interfere with buttonholes. Decorate bands of fabric with your favorite decorative techniques.

To achieve a soutache look, Agnes serges a long chain with heavy threads (such as Decor 6) in both loopers. Then she lays two strands of the serger trim on a

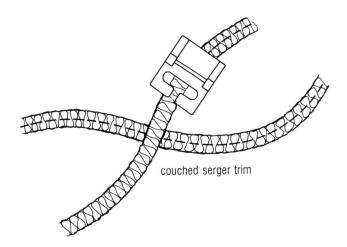

couched serger trim

band of fabric, in a double helix form, couching the strands down with monofilament nylon on her conventional sewing machine.

Agnes invented an unusual technique to highlight the leaf appliqués. First she uses a conventional satin stitch to attach the leaves to the base fabric. Then she outlines the shapes with the same serger trim used for the soutache look. She uses an open-toed embroidery foot to straight stitch the edge of the serger chain with monofila-

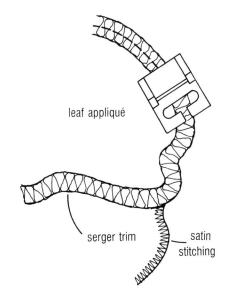

leaf appliqué

serger trim

satin stitching

66

ment thread. The effect is almost three-dimensional.

To apply your decorated bands to the base fabric, create serger piping by folding a 1-1/4" strip of Seams

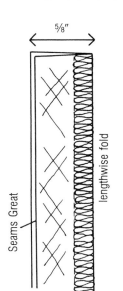

Great in half lengthwise. With a wide rolled edge or balanced 3-thread stitch, stitch over the fold without trimming. Apply the raw edges of the Seams Great to the right side of your decorated bands and seam them next to the rolled edge. Turn the seam to the underside and stitch the band to the base garment, stitching in the ditch.

How-to hints

• Add dimension to the piping described above by serging over filler cord, from 3 to 6 strands of pearl cotton, topstitching thread or the same decorative thread used for the upper looper. A beading foot can help channel the strands together under the stitch.

• Wrap the edge to make a reversible stitch that's great for making serged piping or as a decorative finish.

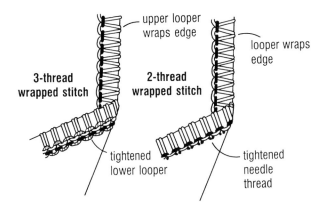

Adjust tensions as you would for a narrow rolled edge, but do not narrow the stitch width. Tighten the lower looper of a 3-thread stitch and the needle of a 2-thread stitch, until the edge is encased. Slight loosening of the upper looper/looper thread may be necessary.

Related page references: for decorative-thread options, see pages 13–19; for decorative-serging basics, see pages 21–31; for flatlocking, see pages 83–91; for serged piping, see page 99; for beading foot, see pages 56, 61–62.

Rather than piecing and seaming to create the color blocks, this textile artist overlays contrasting fabrics and decorative-serging accents. **Created by:** *Agnes Mercik.* **Submitted by** *JoAnn Pugh, Bernina of America.* **Serger brand:** *Bernette.*

Couched cardigan jacket

In his customary exquisite workmanship, Philip Pepper decorates a white linen jacket with flatlocking and a carousel horse appliqué (p.69, left). Philip travels extensively, thrilling people with the fineness of his machine work. Here he uses gold-colored Decor 6 from Madeira in the upper looper (of a 3-thread stitch) and flatlock topstitches, with loops out, along foldlines to make diamondshaped lines on the right side of the bodice. Philip flatlocks yardage 5" wider and longer than the jacket front; then he cuts out the jacket front.

The flatlocking is then decorated with chain, made by threading the upper and lower loopers with Decor 6 and

all-purpose thread in the needle. Philip uses the right needle position and serges about four yards of chain. This is placed vertically over intersecting points on the flatlocked rectangle and couched in place at the intersections and in the middle of the diamond with a single decorative stitch on the sewing machine.

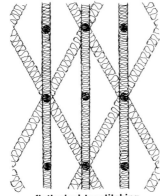

flatlocked topstitching and serged trim

Next Philip makes braid by serging over #3 pearl cotton. Placing the pearl cotton over the front and under the back of the rolled-hem foot helps guide it through. Thread the upper looper with Decor 6, with all-purpose thread in the lower looper and needle. Again, serge 4 yards of trim.

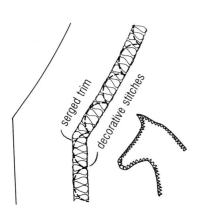

serged trim
decorative stitches

On the left jacket front, Philip uses the 1475CD to appliqué a carousel horse with threads matching the flatlocking. Around the back neck and down the left front and lower edge, he applies the serger trim with decorative sewing-machine stitches.

Couched bolero jacket

Linnette Whicker creates red braid on the serger by stitching a wide balanced 3-thread chain over 5/8"-wide Seams Great, using #5 pearl cotton in the upper looper and all-purpose thread in the needle and lower looper.

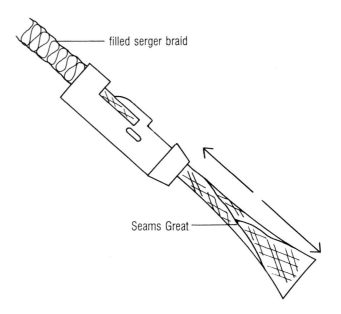

filled serger braid

Seams Great

By pulling the Seams Great toward you, it stretches and narrows, so that it fits under the flatlock stitch, helping hold the full width of the stitch.

How much braid did she make? "Til I was out of thread or Seams Great." This braid is then zigzag couched to a white wool gabardine jacket (p.69, right), using monofilament on top and white thread in the bobbin.

Linnette cut out the pattern and worked flat. She used a quilter's corner template for the design, marking it with a wash-away pen. Then she copied it toward the shoulder and side seams.

How-to Hints

• Try playing with a variety of couched-cord fillers. Seams Great is one option. For an even puffier braid, try crosswise-grain, 1/2" to 1"-wide tricot, cotton interlock or jersey. Cut strips as long as possible to facilitate easier handling and continuous serging. Or, try one or more strands of filler cord: pearl cotton, yarn or satin cord. To assist in glitch-free feeding, use the channeled beading foot, ribbon foot or, for finer filler, a cording foot; also, some all-purpose feet are slotted for cord application.

• If the decorative lines are straight or only slightly curved, you can flatlock the couching braid directly to the project. For more dramatic curves, make the braid separately and apply with conventional sewing, fusing or gluing.

Related page references: for decorative-thread options, see pages 13–19; for flatlocking, see pages 83–91; for serger braid trim, see pages 52, 54–55, 57–59; for cording feet, see page 146.

Textile artists skillfully demonstrate flatlocked topstitching and couched flatlocked braid. **Created by:** *Philip Pepper* (left) *and Linnette Whicker* (right). **Submitted by:** *Louise Gerigk, Pfaff American Sales.* **Serger brand:** *Pfaff Hobbylock.*

Subtle Tone-on-Tone Serging (overleaf)

Serge-finished walking coat

Balanced 3-thread serging, using Ribbon Floss in the upper and lower looper, lends understated style to all edges of this linen-look coat. You can use any pattern with simple lines, but Cindy Cummins's "Coat in a Day" pattern, used here, is already designed for this edging technique.

Cheryl Robinson suggests serging slowly when you use heavier thread. This allows the thread to form con-

sistently and pre-
vents jamming. She
also uses thread
nets to enhance
smooth feeding and
discourage "dump-
ing" around the spool
or cone base.

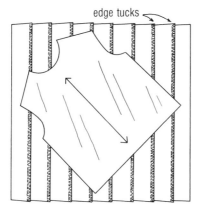

edge tucks

using Sulky rayon thread. She chose a pattern already
designed with tucks, but worked the tucks on the
straight of grain before cutting out the bodice so that the
tucks run diagonally.

Related page references: for ribbon and rayon decorative threads, see pages 14, 19; for decorative basics,
see pages 21–31; for narrow rolled edges, see pages
93–101; for serged tucks, see pages 107, 134.

Tucked dress

Here, Cheryl has
emphasized the
tucks on the bodice
with a rolled edge,

*Cheryl takes an understated approach to decorative serging,
limiting the placements and keeping the color tone-on-tone.
The results? Smart, really wearable looks.* **Created and submitted by:** *Cheryl Robinson, Tacony Corporation.* **Serger
brand:** *baby lock.*

Sprinkle on the Serged Glitz (opposite)

Gold-trimmed coat

On this jaunty polar fleece coat, Nel Howard uses her own technique, called "thread paletting" with Sulky rayon thread.

Behind the serger she puts two to five spools of thread in a jar with a rim. She mixes metallics with coordinating colors and treats them all as one thread in the upper looper. It's easiest to tie all the threads to the end that's already threaded and pull it through, loosening the tension dial.

Pull out an arm's length of the thread and serge. Pause; then pull out another arm's length. This prevents uneven stitches caused by the threads bouncing around in the jar. Occasionally Nel changes just one thread partway through stitching, by tying it onto one of the existing strands. This can change the look dramatically.

Gold-trimmed flower. For decoration, Nel constructed a gold Lycra flower. Start with a single layer of Lycra

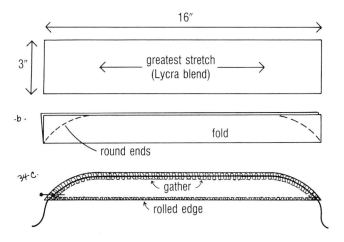

about 3" wide and 16" long. Round the ends so they look like collar bands, with the longest end being at the raw edge. Using metallic thread in the upper and lower looper and regular thread in the needle, finish with a narrow rolled edges, as shown.

On the raw edges, use all-purpose thread in the needle and loopers and serge over heavy thread, like buttonhole twist. Then secure one end of the heavy thread and pull the other to gather the fabric into a rose. You can handstitch the raw edges together to maintain the rose shape or, as Nel has done, use a hot-glue gun to attach them to a stable base (a circle cut from a plastic milk carton works well).

Leaves. To make the leaves, cut leaf shapes from the Lycra and polar fleece. Stretch the fabric as you serge a rolled edge, which will give a pleasing ripply effect.

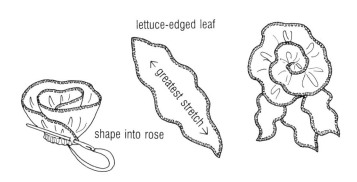

lettuce-edged leaf

shape into rose

greatest stretch

Hand baste the leaves to the fabric and hand stitch the rose above them or glue the leaves to the back of the base. Glue or sew a pin back to the back of the base.

How-to hints

• Consider serged wire applications when making flowers, too. Use a rust-resistant brass, stainless steel or galvanized wire, from light 30-gauge to the heavy 20-

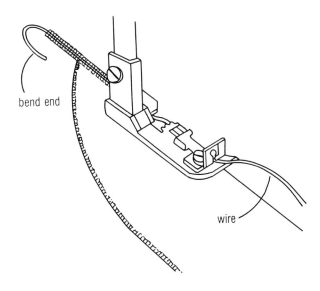

bend end

wire

gauge. Place the wire under the back of the foot, and over the front of the foot, to the right of the needle and the left of the knives. (If you pull the wire strand slightly to the right, it will bump against the lip, and prevent the wire from being cut.) With a beading or cording (for medium to heavier wires) or gimp (for very fine wires) foot, you can guide the strand effortlessly. Test to make sure the wire feeds freely through the foot guides or channels. Start with about a 4" wire tail behind the foot; bend the end into a hook so it won't slip back through the serge-finished edge. Serge over the wire a few stitches, then slip the fabric underneath and continue. Be careful not to crimp and therefore weaken the wire, and hold it just barely above the foot, so it won't obstruct the looper path. Serge off the end, over the wire. Then, with wire snips or crummy scissors, trim the wire to about a 3" tail. Serge off the end. Finish by bending the wires.

• Serge-baste over wire, then push the fabric together to gather. Try this method when gathering the base of fabric-flower petals.

Related page references: for metallic threads, see page 16; for flatlocking, see pages 83–91; for lettuce-leaf edges, see pages 97,120,

With decorative serging and metallic threads, Nel has added glitz to dress up traditionally casual fabric. **Created by:** *Nel Howard.* **Submitted by:** *Juki of America Education Department.* **Serger brand:** *Juki.*

Serged Shag Squiggles (overleaf)

Cocoon shag coat

This detachable cocoon shag collar (p. 74, left) gives a fun yet refined look to any jacket, coat, or cape (including ready-to-wear). The texture is created by making a pile of "shags" with lettuce edging and then applying them to the base.

All fabric is Merino wool jersey ribbing yardage. The lettuce edge on the shags is made by using the differential feed at a "minus" setting, less than 1.

Judy Murphy used Sulky rayon in the upper looper and Woolly Nylon in the lower looper of a 3-thread rolled edge. Since the fabric was heavy and would not wave enough from the differential feed alone, she also applied gentle pressure on the front edge of the fabric as it fed into the machine.

Judy discovered that straight strips did not give a full enough texture. By experimenting, she came up with fig-ure-8-like shapes she refers to as "squiggles." When let-

Judy Murphy accents a black coat and ivory top with serged shag squiggles. **Created by and submitted by:** *Judy Murphy, Stockbridge, Georgia.* **Serger brand:** *White Superlock* (garment at left) *and Viking Huskylock* (garment at right).

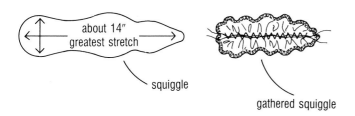

about 14"
greatest stretch

squiggle

gathered squiggle

tuce-edged and applied to the base, these shags curl in a delightful way.

After lettuce-edging all the shags, Judy gathered them on the sewing machine by pulling out the top and bobbin threads, then zigzagging over them down the center of each shag. She pulled up on the threads to gather the shags, then applied them on the base fabric, layering shags one on another. In *Updated Serger Concepts in Sulky®,* Judy also recommends another clever gathering-technique option: setting for the longest straight stitch, changing to a gathering foot, and sewing down the center of the squiggle.

Shag top

The white shag outfit (p. 74, right) is made in the same way, but here Judy has added a complementary sewn embellishment, which she calls "Swiss Cheese Fabric." Using 100% cotton interlock, she cut out the bodice and sleeve pattern pieces. With a fade-away marking pen, she marked points every 2-1/2", offsetting each row like bricks.

At each point, she set a cafe curtain plastic ring and drew around the inner circle. After all circles were marked, she cut out the center, glued the plastic ring in position with Instant Pin, and stitched a free-motion satin stitch over each ring, with Sulky metallic opalescent thread in the top and bobbin. Judy calls this "Charted Needlework in the Round."

How-to hints

• When choosing fabric for lettucing, look for light-to-midweight ribbings and stretchy knits. Cut the length parallel with the stretchier crosswise grain. Remember,

too, that natural fibers—wools and cottons—will usually stretch more than synthetics.

• To increase the amount of lettuce-edge curl, shorten the stitch length, skim rather than trim the edge, increase the presser-foot pressure, and/or widen the stitch bite. If the edge isn't curled enough, or pokies are showing through the serging, try serging again, directly over the first edge finish, without trimming.

• Stretch the shag carefully, from in front of and behind the foot. Too rigorous stretching can bend needles

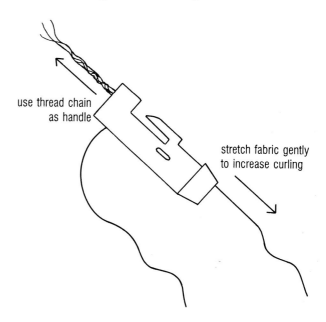

use thread chain as handle

stretch fabric gently to increase curling

and/or inflict looper damage. When starting, use the thread-chain tail as a handle to hold and pull the fabric from behind the foot.

Related reference pages: for rolled-edge, see pages 93–101; for lettuce edging, see pages 97, 120. For more information about Judy's book, *Updated Concepts in Sulky®,* or Sulky thread, see Speed Stitch, on page 154.

Detachable Fishing-Line Ruffles (overleaf)

Gown with detachable ruffles

This stunning taffeta formal has a surprise: the organza sleeves are detachable puffs that can be worn with other party dresses, like the one behind it. The ruffles are finished with a 3-thread rolled edge serged over fishing line, fed through a cording foot. Jonna Harris used Woolly Nylon in the upper looper and all-purpose thread in the needle and lower looper. She rolled both edges of a 6"-wide strip, then gathered down the center

on the sewing machine. The ruffles are attached to an organza base. On both edges of the base are elastic casings.

On delicate fabric like organza, Jonna uses the differential feed set to .7. Every 8"–9" she tugs on the rolled edge to stretch it out over the fishing line, creating the flouncing. Jonna adds, "You will not believe how many yards of ruffles it takes."

Yards and yards of fishing-line flounces can be worn with either dress. Not shown here are matching black gloves, with white ruffles down the length, also made by this serging whiz. **Created by:** *Jonna Harris.* **Submitted by:** *Juki of America Education Department.* **Serger brand:** *Juki.*

How-to hints

• Try different weights of inexpensive fishing line, from 12-pound to 40-pound "test." The heavier the pound weight, the coarser the line. Finer line produces a more ruffled, curled edge, whereas heavier line makes a more flared edge.

• Remember, lightweight, stretchy bias or cross-grain fabric will yield the most curl.

• Allow very long tails—about one-third the ruffle length—at both ends. It will be drawn up inside the flounces when the edge is stretched. The edge can be stretched incrementally, as sections are serged (see p. 76), or after serging the entire length.

• As with feeding any cord or wire under serging, place the fishing line over the front of the foot, and under the back of the foot, between the needle and the knife. A cording or gimp foot will automatically guide the line under the serging.

Related page references: for Woolly Nylon thread, see page 15; for differential feeding, see pages 38–39; for rolled edges, see pages 93–101; for special serger feet, see page 146.

Free-Form Chainstitching and Fringing (overleaf)

Chainstitch-fringed coat

Maximum impact for minimum work: that's what this black wool, unlined, full-length coat offers (p.78). Decorated with various metallic threads of pink, fuschia, purple, gold, and green, the coat is chainstitched in waves on the upper bodice and sleeves. Thread ends are left hanging to add texture. The secret is to choose a simple pattern with no darts or set-in sleeves. The yardage is worked flat either before or after cutting out the pattern.

If the fabric is fine, interface it with fusible tricot interfacing or back it with Stitch 'n' Tear. If you work the design before cutting out the pattern, draw the outlines of the garment pieces on the underside of the wool. Then draw undulating lines from the shoulder area to the underarm and bottom edge areas. The lines stop about half-way down.

Set up your machine for chainstitching. Place metallic thread in the chainstitch looper and all-purpose sewing thread in the needle. For this coat, the looper threads are varied, and include YLI's Pearl Crown, Madeira's Decor 6, and in some places, three colors of Sulky metallic and rayon wound together on a cone and blended as one thread.

With the right side of the coat down, chainstitch along the lines you've drawn. Use the thread release (if available on your machine) to allow you to pull the threads away when you're still in the middle of the fabric. Leave 6" thread tails for the fringe. Pull the top needle thread to the outside, where it will hang with the rest of the thread(s).

Cut out the garment. Keep the focus on the fringe by finishing the edges of the garment with a 2- or 3-thread

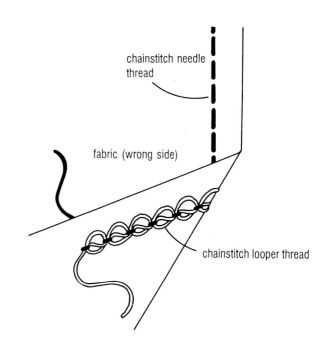

chainstitch needle thread

fabric (wrong side)

chainstitch looper thread

overlock, using black all-purpose thread. Construct the garment on your sewing machine

How-to hints

• Remember, only 5-thread and 4/2-thread models offer chainstitching. See pages 10–11 for stitch configurations and features.

• Because the chainstitch looper does not pass through the fabric, you can safely select from an array of decorative threads: buttonhole twist or topstitching thread, Madeira's Decor 6, Woolly Nylon, blended-thread combinations (as cited in the garment description), and YLI's Candlelight or Pearl Crown Rayon.

Freeform chainstitching and fringing was created by an Elna educational consultant using a 5-thread ElnaLock. To showcase the decorative chainstitch looper thread, the coat was serged right side down. The fringe is simply the thread tails of the double chain-stitch. **Submitted by:** *Andrea Nynas, Elna.* **Serger brand:** *ElnaLock.*

• For the chainstitch needle limit threads to those with a diameter and texture that will feed smoothly and uniformly through the eye and the fabric: serger, all-purpose or topstitching threads work well.

• Remember, the looper side of the stitch exposes the most thread, so serge with the project right side down. (The needle side of the stitch looks like conventional topstitching.)

• For the most impact, keep topstitching and fringing fairly closely spaced. Because the look is free-form, spacing between rows can vary.

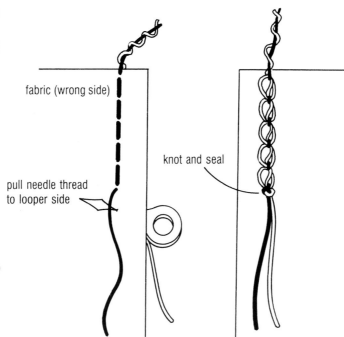

fabric (wrong side)

pull needle thread to looper side

knot and seal

• When making the chainstitch fringe, use a needle threader to pull the needle thread to the looper side, tie and knot it with the looper thread(s), and dab the knot with seam sealant. Trim the thread tails to the length desired.

• As an optional embellishment, consider stringing lightweight bead(s) on the fringe; knot the ends to secure.

Related page references: for decorative-thread options, see pages 13–19; for chainstitching, see pages 10–11; for chainstitched projects, see pages 106, 120.

Patchwork Kimono Coat (overleaf)

Sampler kimono coat

Although you could use denim scraps for this charming garment, Eileen Lenninger uses 3/8 yard each of eight fabrics, including 3-oz. chambrays and lightweight denims. She cuts all the fabric into 6"-wide strips and decorates them with a multitude of serger techniques, using many specialty presser feet. Some are crisscrossed with serger braid, using decorative thread in the upper looper; others use a serger shirring foot to gather the chambray. For the 2-thread rolled hems, she uses a lace foot to guide the edge for flatlocking, she uses the blindhem foot to regulate the stitch width and prevent cutting.

Eileen makes her serger braid with heavy, decorative thread in the lower looper. She covers 5/8"-wide Seams Great with a 3-thread stitch, then fuses it to the fabric and couches it with conventional zigzagging.

When all the strips are decorated, Eileen cuts them into 4", 6", and 8" squares. She repieces the squares, serging them first into strips, then serging the rows together to make new yardage. She cuts the kimono-like coat from this yardage, serging the parts together, then lines the coat.

Related page references: for decorative-thread options, see pages 13–19; for specialty serger feet, see page 146.

serged braid, flatlocked topstitching, and shirring

Eileen texturizes and decorates fabric strips, then serge-seams them into yardage. **Created by:** *Eileen Lenninger.* **Submitted by:** *Louise Gerigk, Pfaff American Sales.* **Serger brand:** *Pfaff Hobbylock.*

Special-Occasion Serging (overleaf)

Red ruffled dress

Cheryl Robinson uses YLI Candlelight in the upper looper to work a rolled-edge on the ruffles. Then to echo the effect, she uses a Sulky metallic thread stitched with a twin needle on the sewing machine. These double lines of stitching crisscross the gathered bodice.

Her lining technique for the skirt is worth learning: Cheryl serges the lining to the bottom edge of the skirt, with a layer of netting in between.

When the lining is turned to the inside and attached at the waist, the netting gives the taffeta skirt body.

Gold lamé and black taffeta dress

Sometimes a serged line acts almost as an accessory, subtly highlighting one part of a garment. For this gown, Cheryl uses Glamour Metallic, with both gold and black threads in it, for the 2-thread rolled edges on the ruffles and bows.

Cheryl says, "I like to think through a pattern, asking myself, How can I enhance this garment with serger techniques?"

How-to hints

• Take advantage of your differential-feed feature when serging lustrous, pucker-prone party fabrics. Adjust for a minus setting, below 1, and if necessary, augment with taut serging.

• Can't find the right shade of metallic thread? Try blending two or three colors together and using as "one."

• Gather ruffles with serging. With

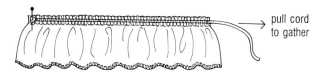

pull cord to gather

your widest, longest 3- or 2-thread stitch, serge over a filler cord, such as buttonhole twist, pearl cotton, crochet thread, or even lightweight fishing line. (A cording or gimp foot is helpful.) Secure one end and pull the other to gather.

• Always, always test and fine-tune decorative threads and stitches on your actual project fabric.

Related page references: for decorative threads, see pages 13–19; for differential feeding, see pages 38–39; for rolled edges, see pages 93–101; for special serger feet, see pages 146–148.

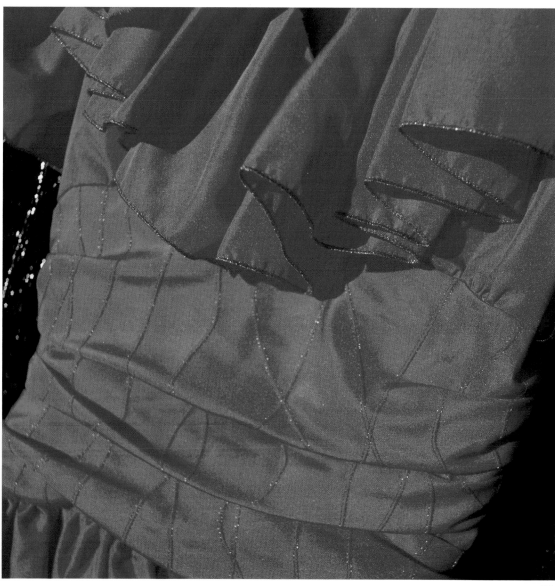

Serging made elegant and easy. Fluid, metallic-thread finished rolled edges lead one to ask: "How did we ever sew without sergers?" **Created by and submitted by:** *Cheryl Robinson, Tacony Corporation.* **Serger brand:** *baby lock.*

Fabulous Flatlocking, from New Basics to Beads!

Flatlocking is serging two layers of fabric together, then pulling them apart until the seam lies flat. Since writing our first book, **Sewing With Sergers**, we have experimented with flatlocking even more and have been amazed by the possibilities!

We'll show you how to flatlock with either a 2– or 3–thread stitch. A 2–thread flatlock will lay flatter, but a 3–thread stitch adds durability.

Woven fabrics can be flatlocked, but they won't be as durable as knits unless stabilized.

For your first flatlocking project, try sweatshirting or polar fleece. These fabrics are easy to sew, inexpensive, and durable.

Flatlocking is Reversible

Depending on whether the fabric is serged right or wrong sides together, there will be **loops or a ladder** (trellis) on the right side.

For **loops** on the right side, flatlock fabric **wrong** sides together. Then pull until the seam lies flat.

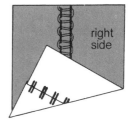

For a **Ladder** on the right side, flatlock fabric **right** sides together. Then pull until the seam lies flat.

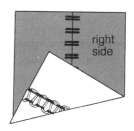

2–Thread Flatlocking

If your machine can sew a 2–thread stitch as shown at the right, you can sew a 2–thread flatlock. Check your manual. Opened flat it will look like the drawings on the bottom of page 0.

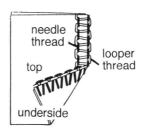

We recommend a balanced tension for a 2–thread flatlock. The needle and the looper threads should meet at the edge of the fabric. If using a heavier decorative thread in the looper, the tension may need to be loosened. Also, if you are flatlocking thick fabrics, both tensions may need to be loosened. Sew a test sample. If the flatlocking doesn't lie flat, loosen the needle and looper thread tensions until both hang over the edge slightly.

3–Thread Flatlocking

The following steps allow you to flatlock with a 3–thread stitch:

1. Loosen the needle tension nearly all the way and tighten the lower looper tension.

2. Do this until the needle thread forms a "V" on the under side and the lower looper forms nearly a straight line on the edge.

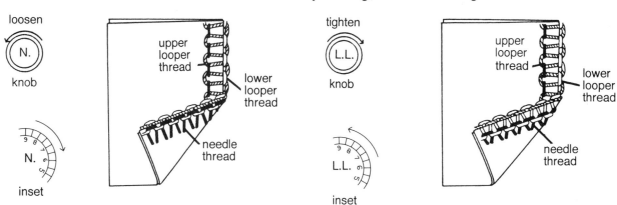

Note: If you have tightened the lower looper tension all the way and still can't get the lower looper thread tight enough, wrap the thread around the tension dial twice. Loosen the tension, then **gradually** tighten while serging **slowly** so you won't bend the lower looper. Some Juki and Bernette serger models have an **extra** tension dial for rolled hems that can also be used for flatlocking. Another option is to use Woolly nylon or a similar texturized thread, or monofilament nylon in the lower looper. It will automatically tighten up the tension dials by two numbers.

Flatlocking will always appear flattest when the loops and the ladder are the same width. IF one side buckles under the stitches, loosen that tension dial. Do not overpress to try to flatten the stitches.

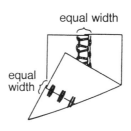

Creative Thread Ideas for Flatlocking

Frame the stitch—When the loops are on the right side, use a contrasting color thread in the needle of a 2–thread stitch or the needle and lower looper of a 3–thread stitch. Your loops will be "framed."

Float the stitch—When the loops are on the right side, use clear monofilament nylon or matching lightweight thread in the needle of a 2–thread stitch or the needle and lower looper of a 3-thread stitch. The loops will seem to be "floating" on top of the fabric.

Define the ladder—When the ladder or trellis is on the right side, it will always be soft because only lighter weight threads can be used in the needle. Try topstitching weight threads for a more defined ladder.

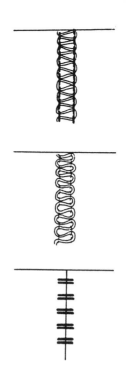

Flatlocking Fabrics that Ravel

It is easiest and neatest to the flatlock on knits because they don't ravel. Even stable wovens may eventually ravel after many wearings and washings. Use one of the following methods to stabilize them:

Method I

1. Sew flatlock seam.

2. Gently pull seam flat and press.

3. Fuse 1" strips of fusible tricot interfacing (such as Easy Knit) to the wrong side, centered over the stitches.

4. If more strength is needed, topstitch from the right side through all layers on both edges of your interfacing. This will prevent ravelling during repeated washings.

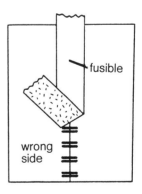

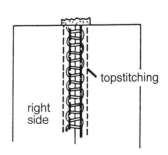

Method II

1. Fold seam allowances to wrong side and press. Serge the edges of the seam allowance.

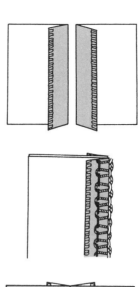

2. Serge the fabric right or wrong sides together, depending on whether you want the loops or the ladder on the right side of the garment.

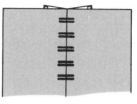

3. Pull the layers until the seam is flat. Lightly press.

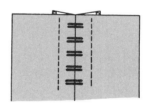

4. As an added decorative touch and for more durability, topstitch the seam allowances flat on both sides of the serging.

How Flatlocking Affects Fit

If you flatlock with the needle in the seamline, then pull the seam flat, the garment width will be increased by the width of the seam allowance or about 1/4"–3/8" per seam.

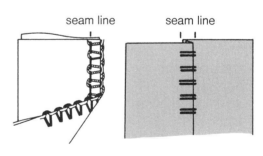

If exact fit is crucial, take a wider seam, increasing it by half the stitch width or about 1/8"–3/16".

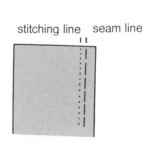

Flatlocking for a Topstitched Look

Flatlock anywhere on a garment. You can even flatlock across flatlocking! Use decorative thread for more stitch definition. This is a great way to dress up sweatshirts or tops **and** to practice your flatlocking.

Fold the fabric and flatlock, being careful not to cut the fold with the serger knives. It is best to only catch part of the fold with the needle so the stitch hangs off the edge slightly. Not only will your flatlocking be flatter, but safer as well—you won't cut the fold. Experiment to see how much of the fold you need to catch in order to get flat flatlocking.

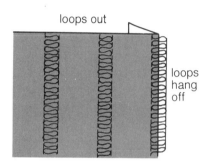

loops out

loops hang off

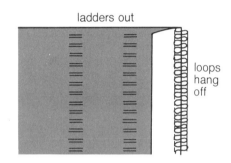

ladders out

loops hang off

Flatlocking Over Ribbon

Flatlock on the fold over ribbon. 1/6"–1/8" width works well because the ribbon should be slightly narrower than the stitch.

This is a great look on blouses and also a pretty embellishment for children's clothes. Apply rows to a bodice or just above a ruffle.

Note: For automatic feeding of the ribbon under the stitch, use a ribbon or tape foot (see page 19).

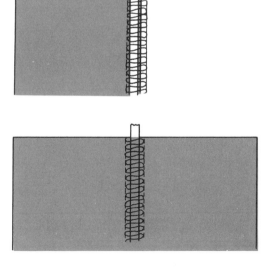

ribbon

Flatlocked Gathering

Narrow, center-gathered ruffles are a nice accent above a flounce on a full skirt or curtains. The ruffle edges can be beautifully hemmed before gathering using a narrow rolled serged hem.

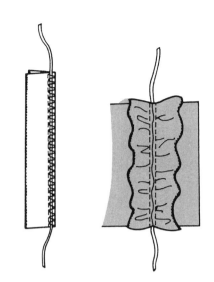

1. Fold fabric in half, right sides together. Serge over cording, being careful not to cut the fold.

   Note: A cording or gimp foot helps feed the cord under the serged stitch (see page 147).

2. Pull up the cord and open the ruffle. Stitch to the fabric on both sides of the cord, or zigzag down the middle with a conventional machine.

Flatlocked Shirring

1. Fold the fabric and flatlock over the elastic cord.

2. Pull up on the elastic. Flatlock shirr your fabric first.

3. **Then** cut out your pattern. This is great for children's clothes.

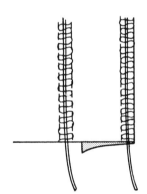
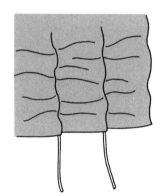

Note: You may find it easier to flatlock first, then thread elastic cord under the loops using a tapestry needle.

Rolled Edge Flatlocking

Change to a narrow rolled edge stitch. Adjust the machine for 2– or 3–thread flatlocking. Flatlock on the fold. The result will look soutache topstitched onto your fabric. "Frame" the stitch by using contrasting color thread as described on page 85.

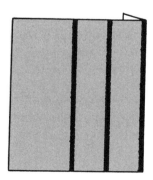

Flatlocked Fringe

This is a wonderful finish for scarves, shawls, skirt hems, placemats, and napkins. It looks great when serged with decorative threads. The Coats & Clark educational staff showed us square wool challis print shawls they had flatlocked with black pearl cotton...gorgeous and much more finished looking than plain fringing.

Choosing the right fabric is a must. How does the fabric look fringed? Is it loosely woven enough to be easily fringed? If not, choose a more suitable fabric. TEST a fringe scrap first.

To flatlock fringe, do the following:

1. Draw a thread to find the straight of the grain on the fabric where your fringe will begin, about 1"–3" from the edge.

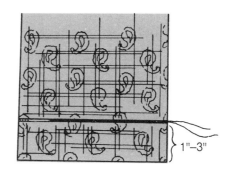

2. Fold your fabric on the drawn thread line.

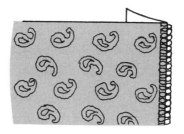

3. Adjust your serger for flatlocking. Test the length and width. Flatlock along the fold of the fabric, with the needle stitching only half way into the fold. The stitches will hang halfway over the edge to allow the fabric to pull flat without a tuck forming underneath the stitching.

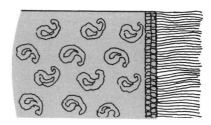

   Flatten the stitches by pulling on them. Then, fringe to the stitching by gently pulling out all threads that are lying parallel to the flatlocking.

Turning Corners When Flatlocking on the Fold

When flatlocking or flatlock fringing, use the following steps for turning corners:

1. Draw threads on all edges to be fringed as described on page 89. Fold the fabric under on the drawn thread line, and flatlock on the fold, beginning where the drawn thread lines intersect. Remember, do **not** cut the fold or your fringe will fall off!

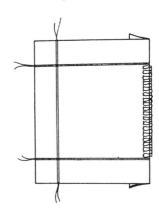

2. When you reach the next drawn thread, raise the presser foot, pull the slack in the needle thread (see page 33), then raise the needle and gently slip the stitches of the stitch finger.

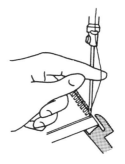

3. Carefully open the first stitching and pull it flat. Fold the next edge under on the drawn thread line. Lower the needle in the top of the first stitching line as shown. **Then**, lower the presser foot and flatlock to the next drawn thread. Repeat these steps until all the edges are finished.

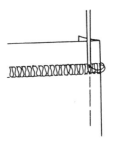

4. On the last edge, stop serging immediately after overlapping the other stitches. Raise the presser foot and the needle. Pull enough slack in the needle to remove the stitches from the stitch finer and pull the fabric from the machine. Allow enough thread tail length for tying and burying under the stitches.

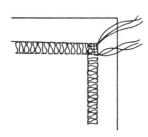

5. Pull the edges flat and fringe to the stitching as shown on page 89.

Flatlock Design Ideas

As a design variation, serge more rows of flatlock topstitching (see page 87) parallel to the flatlocked fringe. Also, vary the look and save time by flatlocking and fringing only one or two sides of a project. For instance, on an oblong scarf, flatlock fringe the short ends first, then finish the longer sides with rolled edges. A skirt hem requires only one row of flatlocked fringing—plus no corners.

Flatlocked Fagoting

True fagoting is accomplished by pulling horizontal threads out of a fabric and tying the remaining vertical threads together in hourglass bunches as shown.

   You can achieve a similar look with the serger. For a delicate hand-crafted look, use this technique to join layers of lightweight cotton or handkerchief linen.

1. Serge to finish seam allowance and press to the wrong side. With the right sides together, flatlock with loops hanging halfway over the edge of the fabric.

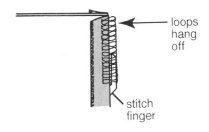

loops hang off

stitch finger

2. When you pull the seam flat, there will be an even width space between the layers.

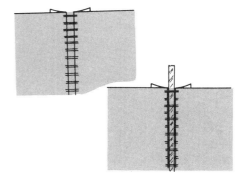

3. Weave a shiny 1/8" satin ribbon in and out of the fagoting as a variation.

Flatlocking over Bead or Pearl Strands

Adjust the machine for the widest, longest, flatlock stitch. Serge over the bead strand (up to 4mm) with the right side of the project on top. The beads peek out of the upper looper, creating a look similar to crocheted beading. If wired bead strands are used, the edge can be shaped—fun!

Raised Flatlocking

To achieve the raised look desired, loosen the needle tension incrementally. Don't loosen the needle tension as much as you would do for a conventional flatlock stitch. This effect is wonderful for wearable art and home accessories.

CHAPTER 9.

Decorative Rolled Edges Made Easy

One of our favorite features on a serger is the rolled edge. Garments like blouses are now easy to sew and professional looking. Save money on children's clothes and use self-fabric ruffles instead of lace. Gail, the home decorating expert, now uses the rolled edge to neatly and quickly finish curtain tiebacks, tablecloths and napkins, and ruffled pillows. Serging is also very durable because the fabric actually rolls under.

Our first book describes rolled edge basics. Now we want to elaborate on the how-tos, the decorative uses of the rolled edge stitch, and the problems you may encounter when venturing on to more challenging fabrics and threads.

Setting Up Your Machine

You will need a narrow stitch finger to sew a rolled edge. On some machines this adjustment is built-in; on others you need to change throat plates. You may also need to change to a special presser foot. Check your manual.

The edge of the fabric actually rolls under because the distance between the knives and the stitch finger is greater than the width of the stitch by at least 1/8".

Set your stitch length to 2mm or shorter if possible. We recommend **gradually** shortening the stitch length until you get the look desired. Most people prefer a satin stitch, but beginning on a very short length may cause uneven feeding of fabric and a lumpy edge. TEST on a sample first!

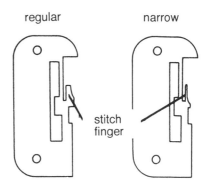

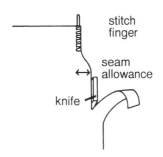

Fabric is always placed on your machine right side up except when serging a fabric that rolls to the right side, like crosswise grain tricot. Why fight it? Place it right side down.

Narrow Edge vs. Narrow Rolled Edge

In machine manuals, you see the terms narrow edge and narrow rolled edge. There is a difference. In both cases the fabric rolls because of the distance between the knife and the narrow stitch finger. However, the narrow edge does roll a bit less, particularlyu on stiffer and/or heavier fabrics. The difference is also caused by tension adjustments.

On a **narrow edge** the stitch is balanced. The upper and lower looper threads of a 3–thread stitch and the needle and looper threads of a 2–thread stitch meet at the edge.

For a **narrow rolled edge**, the stitch is unbalanced. The upper looper thread of a 3-thread stitch and looper thread of a 2–thread stitch encases the edge. Also, the wider the stitch "bite," the deeper the roll.

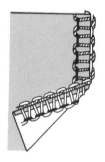
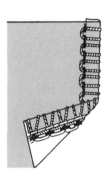

Tension Adjustments for a 3–Thread Rolled Edge

Lower looper—The greatest tension adjustment is on the lower looper. By tightening it nearly all the way, the lower looper thread will become a straight line on the wrong side of the fabric and nearly disappear. It also pulls the upper looper thread to the underside.

tighten lower looper a lot

L.L.

knob

L.L.
4 3 2
0

inset

Note: If you can't get the lower looper thread tight enough, you aren't alone. This is a common problem. In our workshops, our students originally solved this by wrapping the tension dial twice. Do this at your own risk, however, as it is not recommended in the manuals. After wrapping, loosen the tension and begin sewing slowly to make sure you don't overstress the looper and cause it to break. Gradually tighten the dial again if necessary.

The **newer** method of tightening the lower looper tension is to use texturized nylon thread like Wolly Nylon. It automatically tightens the lower looper by two numbers. Monofilament nylon will also tighten the lower looper.

Upper looper—It may need a little tightening or loosening, but it depends on the type of thread and fabric used as well as the stitch length. The softer or lighter in weight the fabric, the more likely you'll need to tighten the tension. Since decorative threads are generally used **only** in the upper looper, TEST on a sample first.

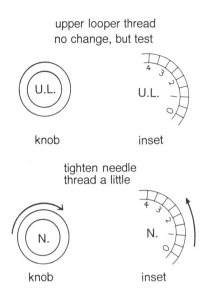

upper looper thread
no change, but test

knob   inset

Needle—The needle thread tends to loosen under the strain, so you may need to tighten the tension. If it becomes too tight, however, the edge may pucker. TEST on a sample first. Puckering most often occurs on the lengthwise grain of fabric.

tighten needle
thread a little

knob   inset

As you tighten the lower looper tension, the upper looper is brought to the wrong side.

As the lower looper become tighter, it creates stress on the needle thread. Tighten it.

Perfect! The upper looper has been pulled all the way to the under side and the needle thread is hidden.

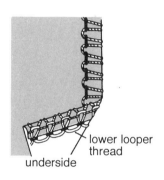

lower looper
thread

underside

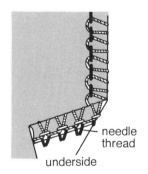

needle
thread

underside

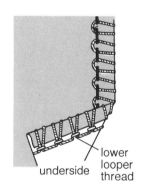

lower
looper
thread

underside

Tension Adjustments for a 2–Thread Rolled Edge

If your serger sews a 2–thread stitch and can make a rolled edge, try it for a lighter edge finish. Bridal veils are often finished this way. Adjust your machine for a rolled edge per your instruction manual.

Tighten the needle tension until the looper thread rolls from the top of the fabric to the underside and encases the edge. If the fabric is heavy, you might also need to tighten the lower looper to make the fabric roll.

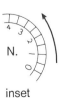

knob   inset

Narrow edge—balanced 2–thread tension

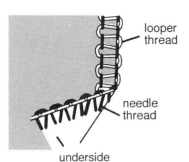

looper thread

needle thread

underside

Narrow rolled edge—unbalanced 2–thread tension

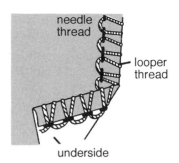

needle thread

looper thread

underside

Decorative Rolled Edges

Make a rolled edge more decorative by using a contrasting or special thread. Rayon, silk, and metallics add shine. Woolly nylon adds texture and provides good coverage. Variegated threads are beautiful because they "color block." Generally, finer threads (extra fine, serger, or regular threads) are softer. However, you can try topstitching thread or Designer 6 rayon for more definition. Pearl cotton, crochet threads, and yarn will generally be too bulky. TEST them using a longer stitch length.

variegated threads

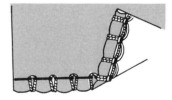

Rolled Edge Stitch Variations

Picot, Shell, or Scalloped Edge
This look, commonly seen in lingerie, is formed by lengthening the stitch to 5mm, 6mm or 7 mm. Serge slowly!! If the fabric puckers, loosen the needle tension. The fabric can be held taut both in front of and behind the presser foot to prevent puckering.

picot, shell or scalloped edge

Blindstitched Scalloped Edge
After finishing an edge with narrow rolled hemming, simply stitch over it with a conventional blindstitch. Allow the zigzag portion of the stitch to stitch just off the edge, pulling it in to form the scallops. (Most machines zigzag to the left, so you will also need to place the rolled edge under the left of the needle.)

blindstitched scalloped edge

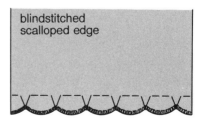

Mini-blanket Stitch

On a 3–thread stitch, loosen the needle all the way and tighten both loopers nearly all the way. Both looper threads will be on the edge of the fabric and the needle thread will show on both sides. Lengthen the stitch to 5 mm. The result will look like a narrow blanket stitch. Try this with lightweight decorative threads in the needle and loopers.

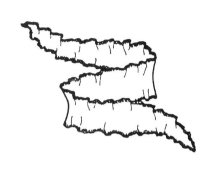

needle
thread

loopers

Lettuce-leaf Edging

This ruffled or "lettuce" effect can be interesting on belts, aerobic wear and skirts. Create a lettuce effect with any narrow or rolled edge set on a short satin stitch length. The degree of ruffling is based on the amount the edge will stretch. The following will affect stretch:

- Using stretchier fabrics such as single knits and jerseys.

- Lightweight fabrics will lettuce more than heavy weight.

- Crosswise grain in knits and bias in wovens will stretch more.

- The shorter the stitch length, the more lettuce effect you will get.

- To increase stretching, increase the presser foot pressure.

Creative Uses for the Rolled Edge Stitch

Rolled Edge Scallops

This technique is great for fabrics or lace.

1. Trim away the seam allowances on scallops.

2. Disengage the knife. If you can't, don't try this technique. Serge the edge of the scallops with a rolled edge stitch. When you reach the inside point between the scallops, straighten the fabric as you would for an inside corner (see page 37). Do not stretch.

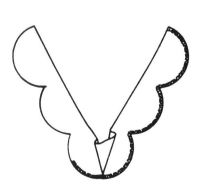

Attaching Laces and Trims

Use the rolled hem stitch to attach laces and trims for a corded edge appearance. Place the lace and fabric wrong sides together and serge with the rolled edge stitch.

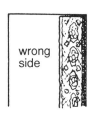

Decorative Belt Loops or Lattice Work

Create decorative strips of fabric for belt loops or lattice work. They can also be woven together for pillows, handbags, yokes, and other accents.

lattice

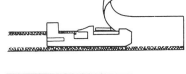

belt loops

1. Cut long strips of fabric 1" wide. Later the strips can be cut into the lengths needed. If necessary, you can interface them to prevent stretch. Fuse the strips wrong sides together with fusible web for extra body and easier handling.

2. Serge along one edge with a rolled edge stitch. Turn the strip around, making sure the same side is on top. Align the first stitching with the left side of your presser foot for even width strips. Serge the other side.

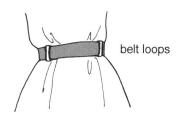

3. Cut the strip into desired lengths.

Sue's Bulk-Free Belt Loop Idea

1. Cut the fabric strip two times the finished width of the belt loop.

2. Fold the fabric wrong sides together, lengthwise.

3. Flatlock the cut edges together with stitches hanging off the edge.

4. Pull the stitching flat. Press.

5. Cut into desired lengths.

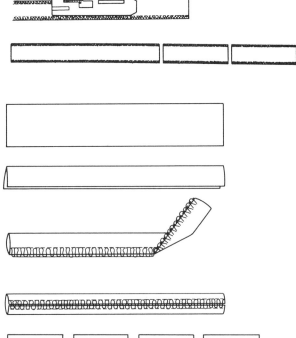

Make your Own Trim

When you can't find trim to match your fabric, make your own. Use lace, eyelets, cotton blends—the sky's the limit!

1. Cut strips of fabric the desired width, plus a seam allowance. If gathering the trim, cut it three times the finished length.

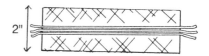

Variation: For reversible trim or ruffles, place two fabric strips wrong sides together before proceeding to Step 2.

2. Serge one edge with a rolled edge stitch. Attach to the garment flat or after gathering.

Create Your Own Piping

By making your own piping with the rolled edge stitch, you will be able to match almost any color of fabric. You can created an unusual lightweight look not available in purchased piping.

1. Cut bias strips of chiffon 2" wide. The bias adds flexibility to the finished piping.

2. Place one to three strands of filler cord such as pearl cotton in the center of the bias strip. Fold bias strip in half over filler cords.

3. Serge over the filler threads with a rolled edge stitch. Trim the seam allowance to 5/8".

Variation: Substitute 1 1/4"–wide Seams Great (bias tricot strips) for the chiffon, and apply the filler cord on top, serging over it. Lay the filler cord down about 1/4" from the right raw edge and serge over it, trimming off 1/4".

You're done! Apply finished piping in a seam or along an edge. Using a zipper foot, stitch close to piping. See our **Sensational Silk** book for complete piping ideas.

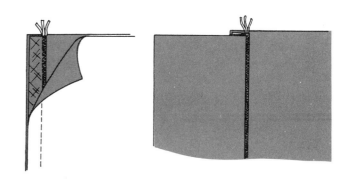

Creative Uses of the Chained Tail Thread

The rolled edge chain itself looks very nice, especially when using a heavier thread like topstitching thread. Every time you use the rolled edge stitch, serge an extra yard for belt carriers, button loops, or spaghetti straps.

Chained Tail Belt Loops
Pull on the chain to smooth out the loops. See our book **Sewing With Sergers** for tips on attaching chain belt loop.

Chained Tail Filler Cord
If you want your rolled hem stitch to be fuller or stiffer, use a matching length of chain as a filler cord. Smooth out excess loops in the chain by pulling it taut. Place the chain on top of the fabric and serge over it with a rolled edge stitch.

Decorative Rolled Edge Seams

Seams Out
Try seaming lightweight fabrics wrong sides together using a rolled edge stitch. Decorative matching or contrasting threads are lovely.

Serge with the two layers of fabric wrong sides together. To prevent raveling, a short stitch length (satin stitch) is best. Be sure to do a "stress test" on a sample. Serge the seam and pull on it to make sure it will hold. Looser fashions will withstand this type of seam the best.

Seams in Sheers and Laces
Rolled edge seams look gorgeous showing through sheers and laces. These are considered decorative because they show. We like to use Woolly Nylon for softness and better thread coverage. Remember to loosen tension for texturized-nylon threads.

To stabilize loosely woven or stretch fabrics, place a 1/2"-wide strip of sheer tricot like Seams Great on top of the seam and stitch through all three layers. Trim the excess tricot close to the seamline when finished.

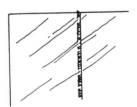

Rolled Edging Over Fishing Line and Wire
Refer to the appendix for fishing line and wire applications.

Solutions to Rolled Edge Problems

Students in our 4-day sewing vacations seem to have some common, recurring problems that we would like to address.

Stitches Do Not Cover the Edge
This is most obvious when the thread and fabric are different colors. Shorten the stitch length; try two strands of regular thread in the upper looper; or use Woolly Nylon as it fluffs and spreads to fill in the spaces between the stitches. Don't forget that you'll need to loosen the tension for Woolly Nylon.

Stitches Pull Away From the Edge of the Fabric
If the fabric is loosely woven, the rolled edge may pull off the fabric. This happens most often on the crosswise grain of the fabric. Lengthening the stitch will help as fewer needle holes will be punched into the fabric. Also, use the smallest needle available for your serger.

Another option is to move the knife farther away from the stitch finger so that more fabric is being rolled into the edge. This can be done on most machines; however, consult your owner's manual. (The adjustment is often called "widening the stitch bite.")

Our last resort is to serge over tricot to stabilize as shown on page 99. Trim the tricot to the serging when finished.

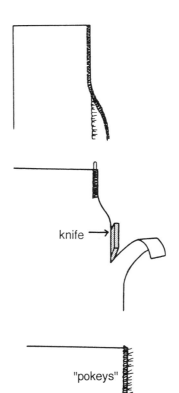

knife →

"pokeys"

The Rolled Edge "Pokeys"
"Pokeys" are little fibers sticking out of the edge, like whiskers. This most often happens with heavier or stiffer woven fabrics that resist rolling. Try widening the bite by moving the knives to the right so more fabric rolls under. Check your owner's manual to see if this is possible.

It is almost impossible to control "pokeys" on metallic wovens. Place a strip of sheer tricot (such as Seams Saver or Seams Great or water soluble stabilizer (such as Solvy or Wash-Away Plastic Stabilizer) on **top** of the fabric and serge through all layers. Trim the excess tricot close to stitching with embroidery scissors, or remove the stabilizer by tearing away or dampening.

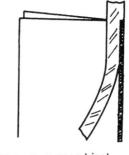

trim away excess tricot

When all other attempts fail, try folding under the raw edge about 3/8" to the wrong side. Align the fold just to the left of the knives. Being careful not to cut the fold, serge along the edge. Using sharp embroidery scissors, trim away the excess fabric to the stitching.

Reverse "Pokeys"

When you see pokeys on the **Inside** of the rolled edge, it means too much was rolled over for the type of fabric you are working with. If possible, move the knives to the left, so more fabric is trimmed. (This is also called "narrowing the stitch bite.")

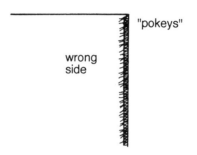

"pokeys"

wrong side

Rolled Edge Puckers

Loosen the needle tension, then try a smaller needle. Also, if the stitch length is too short, the stitches will stack on top of each other and sometimes cause puckers. If you have a differential feed, adjust for a "minus" .5 or .7 setting.

If you do not let the machine trim at least a small amount off the edge, there will be sections with less fabric in the roll, causing unevenness and puckers. Therefore, **always** let the knives trim off a small amount.

Fabric Won't Roll

If the fabric is stiff or heavy, it may not roll. It will scrunch instead, resulting in the "pokeys." Try tightening the upper looper, forcing a roll. If that doesn't work, loosen your upper looper to eliminate the pokeys. However, you will get a wider edge finish.

Rolled Edge is Stiff and Heavy

If you want a lighter rolled edge, use a lighter weight thread such as rayon, silk, machine embroidery thread, or extra fine thread. You can also lengthen the stitch to reduce the density of the thread and use texturized nylon for better coverage if necessary. Or, if available, switch to a more delicate 2–thread stitch.

Rolled Edge is Inconsistent in Density and Width

A rolled edge sometimes looks different in the lengthwise and crosswise grains. There is not much you can do about this (although we have come up with a solution for napkin edges, see page 137). Preshrinking fabric to remove sizing sometimes promotes more even rolled stitching.

The serger always rolls the edge of the fabric down. If your fabric wants to roll up, it will fight the machine and produce an uneven edge. Don't fight it. Place the fabric on the machine so it will roll down.

Also, if you are using a fabric with texture or a bumpy surface such as brocade, eyelet, or pique, there's a good chance your rolled edge will be bumpy, too.

Dog-eared Corners

You can turn corners with a rolled edge, but generally we just serge off, then begin on the other edge, and cross over our first stitching. To secure threads, use a seam sealant on the corners. After it dries, trim off the tails. The sealant is not water-soluble, so the project will be washable, and dry-cleanable.

To avoid dog-eared corners (see top illustration), angle in about 1/8" for the last 1"as shown in the center illustration. Then, on the next edge, begin stitching about 1/8" in from the edge, then angle back (dotted line, lower illustration). The finished appearance, although slightly rounded, appears to be a perfect right-angled corner.

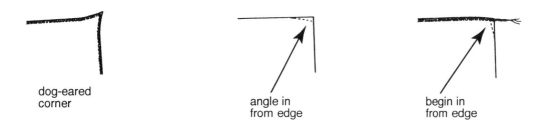

dog-eared
corner

angle in
from edge

begin in
from edge

CHAPTER 10.
Heirloom Serging

The art of French handsewing has been revived and it is all the rage among needle artists. When worked by hand, as it was in the Victorian era, the intricate scheme of lace inserts, pintucks, and entredeaux required hours and hours of painstaking sewing.

In this chapter, we'll show you how quickly and beautifully serging can simulate heirloom sewing. We call it "Heirloom Serging."

You'll love the results for feminine blouses, frilly childrenswear (christening gowns are gorgeous), and on yokes, pockets, or hankies.

Choosing a Pattern

Styles with minimal darting and seaming are best. Also, generous design ease will afford larger garment sections for heirloom serging and less wear stress on the fabric.

Pattern Layout

First, create your heirloom yardage. Then, place the pattern tissue on top of the fabric. Shift the pattern over the stitching to determine the placement that works best. Cut each garment piece single layer. Don't forget to flip the pattern so there will be a right and left side unless the design is asymmetrical.

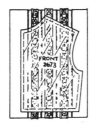  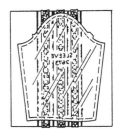

Heirloom Fabrics

Heirloom sewing was traditionally worked on delicate Swiss cotton batiste or organdy. Lightweight wovens such as cotton batiste, organdy, or handkerchief linen are used today. Recommended fabric color choices for heirloom projects are white, ecru, or pastels. Trim and fabrics should be color-on-color such as white-on-white or pale pink on pale pink. However, on white you might add a hint of pastel ribbon or stitching.

Choosing Fine Threads

Finer threads are best for delicate heirloom serging. Try serger or extra-fine machine embroidery thread. A hint of shine from rayon and silk thread can be very pretty. Serge a TEST sample first to check suitability of thread with fabric, trims, and stitches used. Avoid any thread that breaks easily during testing!

Trims, Laces, and Ribbons

Many laces, trims, and ribbons will serge beautifully. When choosing a lace, find one that is soft, but has body; washable, if used in washable garments; the same weight, or heavier than the fabric; and wider than the serger presser foot to avoid bunching. We also like narrow 1/16"–1/8" ribbons under a flatlocked stitch for an accent. The following are some of our favorite laces and trims:

Entredeaux (on-trah-doe)—a trim with 1/16"–1/8"-wide holes similar to hemstitching. For serger sewing choose one with fabric borders. Use it between strips of fabric or other laces and trims.

Beading—can be either a lace or embroidered trim. It has openings through which ribbons can be inserted. Try a narrow pastel ribbon for a hint of color.

Lace Insertion—has a straight edge on each side. Packaged lace seam binding is a common example of lace insertion.

Lace Edging—has one straight edge and one scalloped edge. Use the scallop to finish a hem edge.

Untrimmed Eyelet—makes great lace insertion. The untrimmed edges will be straight after serging. Adjust the finished width of the trim as desired.

Fabric Puffing—made from a strip of garment fabric, gathered on **both** long edges and used as an insertion. For a slightly puffed insert, start with a fabric strip twice the finished length. For full puffing use a strip three times as long. Use the serger gathering technique illustrated on page 88.

Estimating Lace and Trim Yardage

To estimate the yardage of each lace and trim you plan to use, determine the length of each row and multiply by the number of rows. Plus, buy extra yardage for practice and mistakes. The pattern envelope can be of assistance if it gives back length and hem width measurements.

Stitches Used in Heirloom Serging

2– or 3/4–thread rolled edge stitch can be used for:

Inserting laces and trims

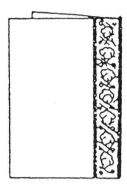

Pintucking (use the width of the presser foot as a guide)

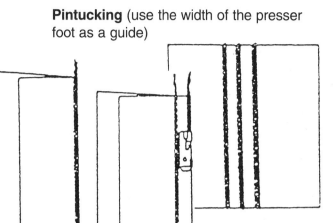

Flatlocking can be used for:

Joining lace to lace, or lace to fabric (loops or ladder can be on the right side)

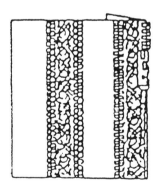

Flatlocking on the fold (generally done with the ladder on the right side)

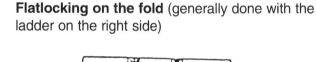

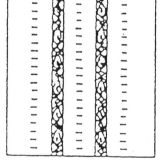

Chainstitch—if your serger will sew a chain, use it to decorate ribbon. With decorative thread in the looper, place the ribbon right side down and sew through the center of the ribbon. Then serge the ribbon to the garment.

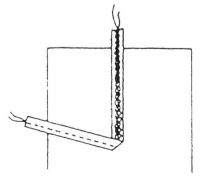

Regular serged seam—can be used for sewing tucks (use a wide width satin stitch) or for joining decorative work.

Decorative stitches on a conventional machine—to fill in spaces between rows of lace or pintucks, use ribbon topstitched in place, or rows of embroidery stitches such as flowers, sewn on a conventional machine.

Creating Heirloom Yardage

It is easier to create heirloom yardage first, then cut out your garment. Estimate fabric yardage the same way we suggested estimating yardage of laces and trims. Add an extra 8" of length for blips and glitches that you'll want to cut away.

If you are creating yardage just for a collar or a yoke, your strips of fabric and trims should be at least 4" longer than the widest part of the garment piece. This allows for shifting of trims as you serge.

The following tips will save your sanity when creating heirloom yardage:

- All stitching should be done on the lengthwise grain to avoid puckering.

- "Test see" a design by laying strips of the trim, lace, and ribbons over the fabric. Rearrange them until you are satisfied. Note the center, spacing, and order of rows.

- Lightly mark the trim placement lines with a water soluble marker.

- Use a foot specially designed for the narrowest seaming and finishing (see page 146).

- Minimize puckering and ensure stitch uniformity by spray starching limp fabric **before** serging.

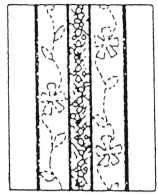
fill in with decorative stitches

create yardage, then cut
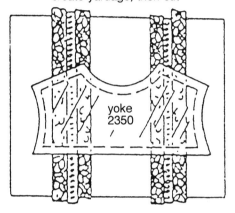
yoke 2350

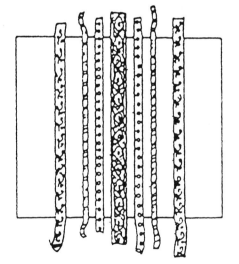
"test see" design

As you build the design, start in the center and add trim to the left, then to the right. Do not build all of one side, then try to repeat it on the other side. Both sides would be guaranteed to look different!

Always sew with lace or trim on top so the upper looper thread is in the same place on both sides. You will sew from bottom to top on one side and top to bottom on the other.

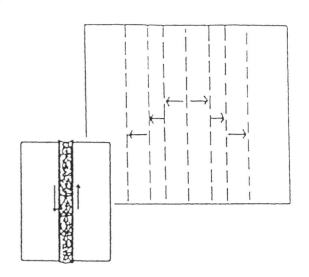

- If you have a stitching problem and need to rip out, remove the entire row of stitching. If the stitching is on the fold like pintucking or flatlocking, be careful not to cut the fabric. A hole will make the area too weak to hold up after restitching.

Heirloom Serging Order

The following is a sample of a sewing procedure used to create heirloom yardage:

1. Draw the center line and insertion lines on the fabric with a water soluble marker.

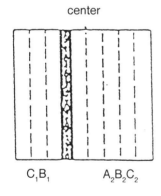

center

C_1B_1 $A_2B_2C_2$

2. Cut on line A and insert the trim.

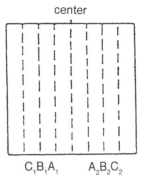

center

$C_1B_1A_1$ $A_2B_2C_2$

3. Cut on line A2 (see Step 2) and insert the lace.

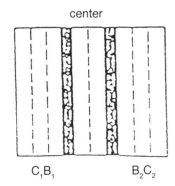

center

C_1B_1 B_2C_2

4. Cut on line B1 (see Step 3). Insert the trim and trim. Then cut on line B2 (see Step 3). Continue until all the trim has been inserted.

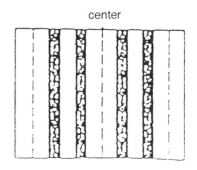

center

CHAPTER 11.
Decoratively Serged Sweatshirts (& Tops)

Sweatshirts are easy, fast-to-finish projects. What other garment could be serged decoratively in so many different ways? Sweatshirt fabrics are easy to handle and popularly priced! They hold their shape but are flexible enough to "forgive" less-than-perfect serging and fitting.

Don't have time to sew a sweatshirt? Combine decorative threads and stitches to jazz up plain ready-made sweatshirts available in both set-in and raglan sleeves and in a wide range of colors.

Note: Remember, too, that most of the techniques and tips in this chapter apply to any knit top.

The Patterns

All the pattern companies now offer sweatshirt styles for women, men, and kids. Sweatshirt patterns are usually designed with few seams. Unseamed areas on the front and back provide a large area for decorative serging. Even the most basic pullover style can be transformed into a designer sweatshirt.

The Fabric

Sweatshirt fleece can be cotton, cotton/polyester, cotton/acrylic, 100% acrylic, or 100% polyester. Always preshrink sweatshirt fabrics by washing and drying the fabric **twice** before cutting out your pattern. This prevents "progressive" shrinkage. Use laundry detergent to remove any excess sizing and dye.

The Ribbing

A wide variety of ribbing is finally available to the home sewer. Ribbing choices are many— 100% cotton, cotton/Lycra, cotton/polyester, nylon, acrylic, acrylic/polyester, acrylic/wool, and 100% wool. The ones that are most resilient are cotton/Lycra (incredible stretch recovery, but hard to find and less ribbed looking), 100% nylon (can be "plastic" feeling), acrylic/wool (the more wool, the more resilient), and 100% wool (gorgeous, versatile, and spendy). The following are tips for purchasing ribbing:

The key to the right ribbing is that care requirements for the ribbing and garment should be the same.

Avoid sloppy ribbing by TESTING resiliency. Simply stretch the ribbing firmly. Does it return to its original size? If not, look for another. Words of wisdom from our ribbing expert, Naomi Baker, "Ribbing that stretches out and doesn't stretch back will **always** be ugly no matter how well you sew."

Combine similar weight fabrics and ribbings.
If the ribbing is heavier, it will overpower the
fabric. If the ribbing is too lightweight, it won't
have the body and resiliency to control the edge.
Our favorite ribbing/fabric combinations are wool
ribbing on wool doubleknit or silk charmeuse.
We also like cotton/polyester ribbing on cotton/
polyester interlock knit. If you can't find a heavy
enough ribbing, use a lighter weight double
layer. Experiment!

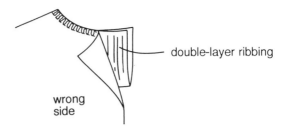

wrong
side

double-layer ribbing

Know how ribbings are sold. The most commonly available are 24"–60"-wide tubular **ribbings
sold by the yard**. 1"–4"-wide **ribbed bands** with one finished edge are also available and often
coordinated to yardage. Gail's favorite finish for crew neckline tee-shirts is a ribbing band folded
wrong sides together and applied double layer for extra body. Rib knit collars are real timesavers,
and not for polo shirts only.

Often striped or finished with interesting edgings like picots, rib knit collars are great for
perking up a solid color fabric. Buy three collars—one for the neckline and two for the cuffs.

Be sure to check the previous cut edge on a bolt of ribbing. Purchase enough to allow for
squaring and straightening.

Be creative if you can't find MATCHING ribbing. Consider contrasting colors. Black is elegant
on most brights. White is a nice accent on a print. Gail salvages ribbing by trimming it off worn or
outdated clothes (some are thrift shop finds). She also knits her own ribbing, especially nice for
heavy woolens, leathers, or leather-likes.

Do not preshrink ribbing. Preshrinking ribbing makes it soft and much harder to handle. Only
lengthwise shrinkage will occur if any, not significantly affecting the stretch or fit.

**Ribbing ratios mean the ribbing should hug the body and keep the edge of the garment
from stretching.** Generally, all ribbing is stretched at least a little when applied, even to a straight
edge. The more curved the edge, the more you will need to stretch the ribbing to make it lie flat
and hug the body. Knowing how much to stretch ribbing becomes intuitive for ribbing enthusiasts.
Unfortunately for beginners, there are no absolute rules, because there are too many variables.

Ribbing that is stretched too much—causes puckers in the neckline of the garment.

Ribbing not stretched the right amount—stands away from the body.

Ribbing stretched the right amount—hugs the body.

Round necklines—Cut ribbing 2/3 the size of the neckline and pin in place distributing ease evenly.

Oval necklines—Cut ribbing 3/4 the size of the neckline. Place most of the stretch over the shoulder area. For 5"–7" across center front and back, stretch ribbing only 1/2"–1".

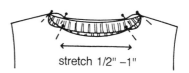

stretch 1/2" –1"

For "V" necklines—Cut ribbing 3/4 the size of the neckline and stretch only slightly down the front.

For turtlenecks—Cut the ribbing the same size as the neckline or slightly less if very tight.

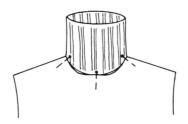

Make sure ribbing will fit. Common sense is a good guide for fitting ribbing. Simply pin the ribbing into a circle and try it on. does it fit easily over your head, wrist, or waist.

Serging Ribbing—Sue's Favorite Tips

- **Use either a 3– or 3/4–thread stitch** because they have the most give. Use a medium stitch length and medium to wide width.

- **Lift the presser foot** and put the layers of ribbing and fabric under it. Lower the presser foot and begin sewing.

- **Always serge with the ribbing on top**, with the exception of "V" necklines. See page 115.

- **Follow a flat construction sewing order** to avoid serging in a circle. See pages 45 and 117.

- **When applying ribbing over other serged seams**, reinforce those seams for 1" on a conventional machine. Since a narrow seam allowance is used to apply ribbing, seams can "pop" where they meet ribbing.

- **Trim all seam allowances on ribbing and garment to 1/4"**. This makes it easier to apply ribbing evenly.

- **If you goof, rip out stitches** or in many cases, can serge again, trimming off the first seam. It will make your ribbing narrower, however. You can also serge over first stitching to even up an uneven seam.

- **Press minimally**. Touch the iron to seam allowances only. Pressing can stretch some ribbing. Press over a ham, steaming the ribbing to shape of neckline. Let ribbing cool before moving.

- **Do not use seam sealant** to secure the ends of neckline ribbing seams. When it dries, it be scratchy! Gail discovered this when her daughter, Bett, complained. Knot close to the fabric instead (see page 34).

Circular Ribbing Application

This is the most common ribbing application, popular to Tee-shirts and also used on cuffs and waistlines. Our students prefer this tidy technique. The ribbing is seamed in a circle first, then serged on.

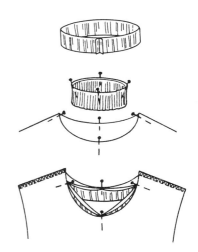

1. Cut the ribbing to size.

2. Right sides together, seam the ribbing into a circle with conventional straight stitch. Finger press open.

3. Fold ribbing wrong sides together. To distribute ease evenly, quarter both ribbing and neckline.

4. Match the pins and serge, stretching ribbing to fit garment edge. **Remove** pins as you serge.

5. To end the seam, overlap stitches for about 1"–2", then taper off the edge.

Ribbed "V" Necklines

1. Serge one shoulder seam.

2. Serge ribbing to neckline with fabric on top to ensure catching the "V." Use the inside corner technique on page 37.

3. Miter the "V" by folding it in half along the center front. Machine baste on a conventional machine from the serged needle line to ribbing edges. From the right side, make sure the ribbing seams and edges match. Then final stitch with a straight stitch.

4. Clip the miter fold and press back. Hand tack the raw edges flat to the serged seams.

5. Finish garment using crew neckline sewing order.

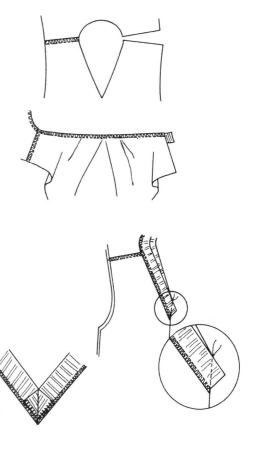

Creative Ribbing Ideas

- Lettuce the top edge of double-layer ribbing.
  Use a narrow rolled edge and texturized
  nylon such as Woolly Nylon thread. Stretch
  as you sew. Lettuce leaf ribbed socks to
  match!

- For the Esprit look, mix and match ribbing
  colors on top.

- Pants or top too short? Serge ribbing to the
  hem edge. Instant fashion.

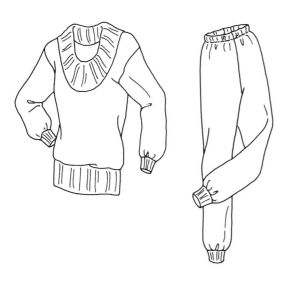

- Layer contrasting color ribbing at the neckline or cuff. The underlayer peeks out,
  forming a border.

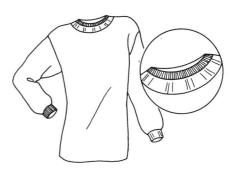

- Ribbing tip: remember, **not** using hipline
  ribbing, but simply serging, turning and
  topstitching may be the most slenderizing
  line.

Thread Possibilities for Creative Sweatshirts

Because most of us wash rather than dryclean sweatshirts, decorative threads, yarns and ribbons used should withstand repeated washing and drying. Among the most durable are topstitching thread, crochet cotton, and texturized nylon such as Woolly Nylon.

Helpful Notions

There are several notions you will find helpful when creatively serging sweatshirts, including a water-soluble marking pen, ruler, and dressmaker's curve, seam sealant, a seam ripper, and loop turner.

The Stitches

Several decorative stitches are appropriate for sewing creative sweatshirts. Our three favorite stitches for sweatshirts are:

Flatlock Stitch (page 84)

Framed Flatlock Stitch (page 85)

Serged and Lapped Seam

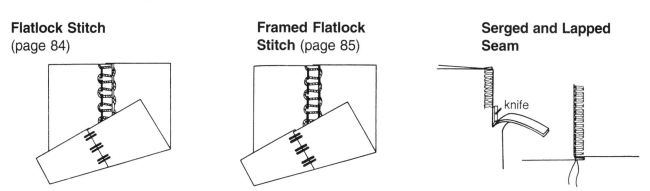

Note: To make a decorative serged and lapped "flat-felled" seam, serge fabric wrong sides together with a balanced wide, medium-length stitch. Press seam to one side with decorative thread on top and topstitch seam flat through all layers on a conventional machine.

Decorative Serging Order for Raglan Sleeves

1. Serge all but one back sleeve seam.

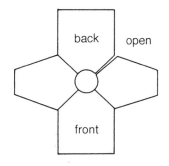

2. Add decorative serging. Try one of these ideas:

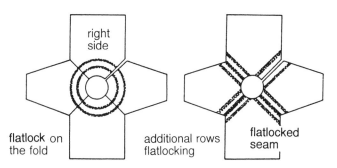

3. Then serge ribbing to neckline and sleeves.

4. Serge the back sleeve seam through neck rib.

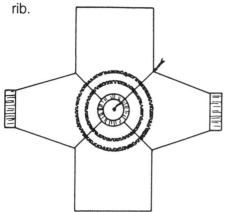

5. Serge one underarm seam.

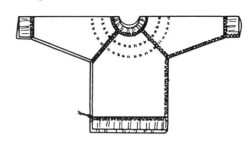

6. Serge the ribbing to the hem.

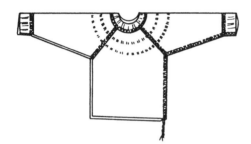

7. Serge other underarm seam.

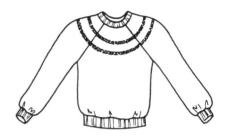

Decorative Serging Order Set-In Sleeves

1. Decoratively serge pieces. Sew one shoulder seam. Apply the neck ribbing.

2. Serge the other shoulder seam. Set in the sleeves. Apply the sleeve ribbing.

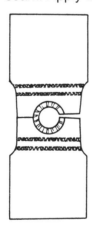

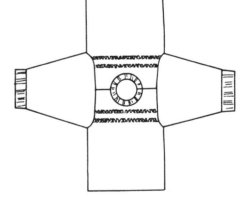

3. Serge one underarm seam. Apply the lower ribbing.

4. Serge the underarm seam.

The "Ski Sweater" Sweatshirt

Using your favorite raglan sleeve sweatshirt pattern, you can make a plain sweatshirt into a "ski sweater." A basic ready-made raglan sleeve sweatshirt is simple to decorate. Consider different colors of thread on the same shirt.

Flatlocked rows.

Flatlocked rows alternating with decorative stitching sewn on a conventional machine.

Flatlocked seams in a color blocked design.

Ribbings attached with decorative "flat-felled" seams.

More Creative Knit Ideas

Lettuce-Edge Ruffling

1. Try on the shirt and mark the lettuce line first with pins. Then mark the line with a water soluble marker.

2. Fold the sweatshirt, wrong sides together, on the marked line.

3. Stretch the folded fabric and serge with a roll hem stitch.

Fastest Color Splicing Ever

1. Use a striped fabric and flatlock along stripes.

2. Then cut out the sweatshirt and sew it together.

Random Flatlocking

Flatlock stitch at random on fabric before construction.

Flatlock Piecing

Use the same flatlock technique for small areas such as yokes. Mark first with a water-soluble marker. Flatlock squares that are cut on the bias.

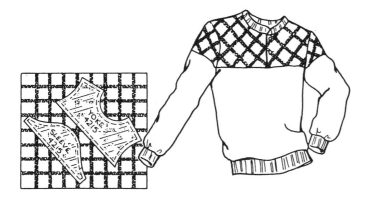

CHAPTER 12.
Quick Patternless Accessories

Need an accessory to wear tonight or give tomorrow? Take your pick! Serging makes them incredibly fast.

Flatlocked and Fringed Accessories

Our serger workshop students **love** our scarves and shawls with flatlocked and fringed finishing.
Experiment with decorative threads, yarns, or ribbons. For heavier fabrics like wools and boucles, consider yarns, pearl cotton, or easy-to-use buttonhole twist/topstitching thread. When flatlocking silks, Gail likes rayon thread or Woolly Nylon.

Large Scarf or Shawl

Flatlock and fringe all sides with a fringe depth of 1/2"–1 1/2".

Suggested fabrics—printed scarf "squares" in rayon or wool challis, silk or silk-like faille, or charmeuse, or lightweight boucles.

Yardage required: 40"–60" square; for 40" x 40" size, 1 1/8 yard of 45" + fabric. For 60" x 60" size, 1 2/3 yard of 60" width fabric.

Muffler

Flatlock and fringe the short ends (depth, 1"–3") before finishing the long sides with narrow rolled or decorative serging.

Suggested fabrics—light- to medium-weight wools, wool blends, or acrylics (good for sensitive skin!).

Yardage required: 1/4 yard of 45"–60" width fabric.

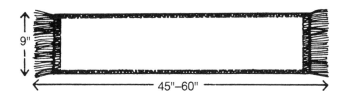 

9"

45"–60"

Ties and Sashes

Flatlock and fringe the short ends before finishing the sides with narrow rolled serging. Braid three ties together for an unusual look.

Yardage required: 1/4 yard of 60" fabric; 1/2 yard of 45" or wider fabric (piece in center).

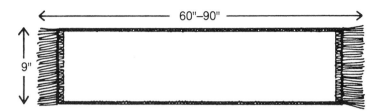

Reversibles

Line flatlocked and fringed accessories with lighter weight fabric in a contrasting color. Fringe the single layers first. Then place the wrong sides together. For square scarves, straight stitch the two layers together about 1/8" in from the fringing. For oblong mufflers, ties, and sashes, fringe the short ends of both layers, then serge the longer edges together using a decorative narrow rolled edge.

Yardage required: 1/4 yard 45"–60" width fabric for both fabric and lining.

Note: See our book, **Sewing With Sergers**, for other scarf sizes and styles.

Chainstitched and Serged Belt

Sewing journalist and consultant Janet Klaer, formerly of Coats & Clark, showed us a nifty belt that can be sewn entirely on a serger. Use contrasting color lining to create a reversible belt. (You need a serger that will sew a chainstitch.)

Suggested Fabrics—Light- to medium-weight fabrics like linen or linen-likes and silks or silk-likes.

1. Cut two belt pieces, about 3" wide by your waistline measurement plus 16". For waist sizes up to 29", 45" width fabric affords enough length for a belt. For thicker waists, piece with a serged seam to achieve the desired length.

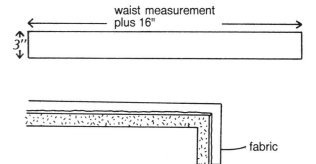

2. Sandwich a layer of polyester fleece between the wrong sides of the fabrics.

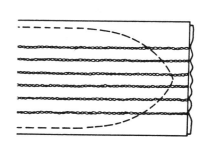

3. With a 4/2-thread chainstitch, channel quilt the layers together, alternating stitching direction to prevent grain distortion. To keep rows even, use the presser foot width as the distance between rows. Try using pearl cotton or other decorative thread in the looper and stitch the belt right side down.

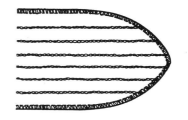

4. Finish the belt edges fast with 2– or 3–thread narrow rolled or balanced serging. If decorative thread was used for chainstitching, use the same thread for the edging and taper the ends.

One-Size-Fits-All Belt

This versatile belt is made from a strip of synthetic suede, such as Ultrasuede, Ultrasuede Light, Facile, or a dressmaker-weight leather. The belt can be worn either with the ends in or out.

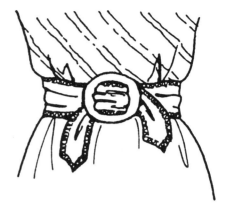

1. Cut a piece of fabric 1/4 yard wide by a least 44" long. Add body by making the belt a double layer. Except for true leathers, you can fuse the layers together with fusible web. One layer can be a contrasting color.

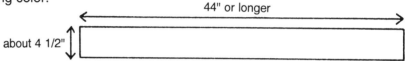

about 4 1/2" | 44" or longer

2. Finish the long edges with decorative serging.

3. Square, taper, or round off the ends as desired.

square

tapered

rounded

4. You're almost finished. Thread the belt ends through a buckle, one at a time. Adjust it to fit. The belt can be worn with the ends in or out.

completed belt
(worn with ends in or out)

Soft Tote in Seconds

1. Finish the edges of three 16" squares with narrow rolled edge serging. Durable, tightly constructed cotton or cotton blend wovens work best.

2. Straight stitch the scarves right sides together, using a 1/8" wide seam allowance along the serged needle line.

3. Assemble as shown. Tie the unseamed corners into a square knot.

Great for toting knitting, kids' toys, beach attire, or gym clothes!

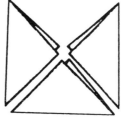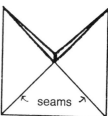

seams

CHAPTER 13.
Creatively Serged Aerobic and Swim Wear

More and more home sewers are serging leotards, tights, and swimsuits. The increased interest is no doubt due to the popularity of serging. The Palmer/Pletsch Sewing Vacation students marvel at serging leotards in an hour or less. After mastering the basics shown in **Sewing With Sergers**, move on to these creative serging ideas.

We like Woolly Nylon thread or similar brands (see page 15) best for serging aerobic and swim wear because it is very strong and holds the seams well. Plus, it is soft...great for body fitting fashions.

Inside-Out Fashion

Aerobic or swim wear can be worn wrong side out! The serged elastic application looks like flatlocking when worn on the outside. All the rage among the Jane Fonda set, these leotards can also be worn right side out for a more traditional look.

Use contrasting thread. Experiment with different stitch widths and lengths...generally a medium to wide balanced stitch works best. For more color density, serge again over the first stitching.

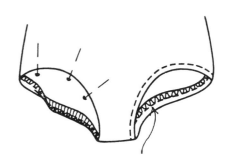

For armholes, necklines, and leg openings, serge the raw edges with the contrasting color thread, turn up, and topstitch the elastic casing. Or, use the ready-to-wear technique specially designed by Palmer & Pletsch for McCall's patterns that allows you to serge elastic to the raw edge, then turn up and topstitch. See **Sewing With Sergers** for the complete instructions.

Serge the side seams with the same contrasting color thread. They become quite narrow in stretchy aerobic wear and look more like a design line.

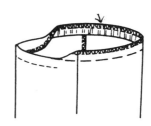

serge twice
for thread density

Note: To prevent jamming and thread build-up, adjust for the longest-length stitch before seaming the elastic to the garment. (The stitch will be "shortened" when the elastic relaxes.)

More Design Ideas

Line two-way stretch leotards and swimsuits with the same fabric in a contrasting color. The additional layer doubles the wearing mileage, smoothes the figure, and makes the garment reversible. Sew the fabric and lining separately. Place the two layers wrong sides together and join when applying elastic to the edges.

- **Try a double needle** for topstitching the elastic casing. It is more durable and a great look—often seen in ready-to-wear!

- **Lettuce edge** belts, ruffles, and necklines (see page 97).

- **Add ruffles** to a neckline or insert them into a seam. Finish with a rolled edge stitch (see page 96).

- **Color block** or splice tights. Teens love different legs! This look is wild and the price is right; for most, only one yard of fabric is required. Using strong Woolly Nylon thread, flatlock the color-spliced seams to minimize bulk.

  Note: Another look popular with the aerobic set is stirrup-less capri length tights that can also be color blocked. Simply trim the stir-rups off and finish the bottom edge with a serged satin stitch.

- **Two-way stretch fabrics make gorgeous pareos**. Buy an extra 1–1/4 yards of your swimsuit fabric. Finish the edges with narrow rolled satin serging. Tie on for an instant dress or skirt, as shown.

Aerobic Headbands

All exercisers—golfers, tennis players, and joggers—love sweatbands. Fishermen and hunters are kept warm with wool headbands. Serge them by the dozen—fast. Use prefinished ribbing, ribbing yardage, or two-way stretch fabrics. Buy fabric or recycle ribbing about 12" long and 2"–3" wide (the stretchier, the better). Vary the style with the type of ribbing used.

Two-way Stretch Fabric Headbands
These headbands are easy to make because they only require one seam and can double as pull-on belts (for small waists only!). Use cotton/spandex (Lycra) blend knits for comfort and absorbency.

1. Cut two pieces of two-way stretch fabric as shown.

2. Loop the pieces of fabric together. (Don't worry about the raw edges—the knit doesn't ravel and automatically curls under like an instant hem!) Place the ends of each loop wrong sides together. Stretch to fit your head and mark the seamline.

3. Serge the four layers together.

Medium-Weight Ribbed Headbands
1. Fold ribbing in half length wise, wrong sides together. Flatlock the seam (see page 86) and pull flat.

2. Stretch it around the wearer's head until it is snug, but comfortable. Mark the seamline and serge. For variety, add a twist before seaming as shown.

Medium- to Heavy-Weight Headbands
Note: This type of ribbing has one finished edge.

1. Cut a single layer and finish the one raw edge with medium-to-wide balanced serging. Trim at least 1/4" off the raw edge while serging to prevent stretching.

2. Stretch to fit the head, mark the seamline and serge.

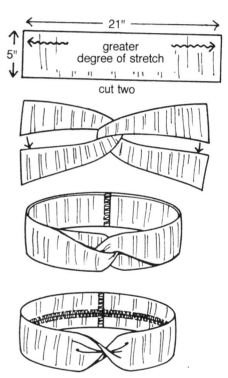

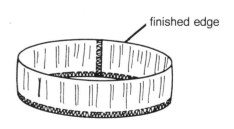

finished edge

CHAPTER 14.
For Kids—Serge it Fast (and Creatively!)

When it comes to kids' clothes, sergers are indispensable. Finally, you'll sew fast enough to keep up with those fast growing bodies.

The childrenswear you serge instantly (well, almost!) will look better and last longer than any ready-mades. Both Pati (daughter Melissa) and Gail (daughter, Bett and son, Jack) have noticed that their serged "custom-mades" stand up to repeated washings!

Serger Shortcuts

Replace bindings on jackets and vests with decorative serging. If the garment is reversible, use a stitch that looks the same, or is decorative, on the upper and lower looper.

Create your own trim—the cost savings are substantial. Finish one or both of the edges with a narrow rolled edge. If there is enough fabric, cut the fabric strips on the bias for softness and stitch uniformity. For ruffles, gather on a conventional sewing machine (we like special ruffler attachments or gathering feet). Or, if the fabric is lightweight, gather on the serger (see page 88), with or without a shirring foot (see page 146).

Shirr with serging. Thank goodness Sue Green developed this technique—it's the only shirring Pati or Gail have time to finish. Shirr the fabric before cutting out the fabric. (See page 88).

Make Frilly Blouses and Dresses Fast!

Pin tucks are perfect. Experiment with fine, shiny threads like rayon, and different stitch lengths.

1. Tuck the fabric before cutting it out.

2. Press mark the tuck fold lines.

3. Plan the serging direction so the top side of the stitch will always show on the right side. Remember, too, that the lengthwise grain will serge more uniformly and smoothly than the crosswise grain.

4. Disengage knife, if possible.

5. Serge along the foldline with a narrow rolled edge or a narrow balanced stitch.

draw lines   finished pintuck   serge on fold

Quick-to-Serge Kidswear Ideas

Serge children's swimwear, leotards, and tights. Chances are if you've sewn your own, there will be enough yardage left over for a wee one.

Serge Halloween get-ups! Buy preprinted costumes that glow in the dark. No more facings or bindings. Anxious Halloween goblins love the super-fast process.

Serge reversibles. Simple silhouettes like tee-shirts and jumpers are perfect candidates. (See page 129.)

Baby's Bounty

Serged diapers! Choose super absorbent 100% cotton terry (preferred in England where they're called "nappies"), special diaper flannel, or knits. Simply serge finish the edges. Use two to four layers, depending on the fabric weight.

Sizes 11" x 13 1/2" for infants to nine months. 13 1/2" x 16 1/2" for toddlers. Also, look for the many new, contoured diaper patterns now on the market—most include serging instructions and are very fast to make.

As a starter set, most babies need at least three dozen or about 2 1/2 yards of 45" fabric for infants and 5 3/4 yards of 45" fabric for todlers.

Serge Blankets!

Look for 100% cotton flannel or soft acrylic sweaterknits. An ample size is 45" x 45" or 1 1/4 yard of 45" width fabric. For newborn babies, 30" x 40" receiving blankets are nice. Make them double if using flannel. Finish the edges with baby yarn in the upper looper. Or use #8 pearl cotton in both upper and lower loopers.

Blanket Variations!

Add a protective hood to one corner. When made in terry cloth, this is the perfect after-bath "robe."

Flatlock satin blanket binding or ribbon to the edges. Pati's daughter Melissa adopted a satin-edged blanket as her favorite.

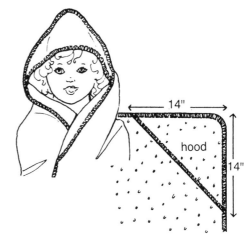

Our Favorite No-Tie Bib

You'll need one fringed guest towel about 11" x 18" and 2" wide and cotton or cotton blend ribbing that is about 16" in length.

1. Fold the guest towel as shown. Trim out the neckline opening using a large cereal bowl as a guide.

2. Cut the ribbing 4"–5" shorter than the neckline edge measurement but large enough to fit over the child's head (see page 113).

3. Seam the ribbing and serge to the right side of the neckline, evenly distributing the towel ease (see page 113.)

Note: If you use a larger towel, the bib becomes an after-bath cover-up.

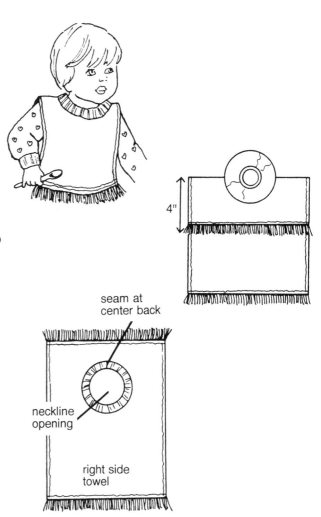

CHAPTER 15.
Serged Home Decorating and Crafts

No time to sew? Satisfy your creative urges and make your home more beautiful with these super-fast-to-serge projects.

Napkins

Somehow **cloth** napkins transform any meal into a dining occasion. Plus, serging napkins is a productive way to perfect decorative stitching, particularly the rolled edge. Gail's **first** serger project was 75 napkins...every one was serged with a different thread or tension to experiment with the various looks.

There's not an easier-to-make nor more welcomed gift than cloth napkins. Dive into your fabric stash...good chance there's a cotton or cotton blend perfect for napkins. Unlike 100% synthetic ready-mades (Pati's pet peeve) they'll really absorb!

Yardage Estimates	Fabric Widths		
	Quantity	45"	54"–60"
18" x 18" (dinner size)	Four Six Eight	1 yard 1 1/2 yards 2 yards	1yard 1 yard 1 1/2 yards
15" x 15" (size of most ready-mades and the most economical to make from 45" width fabric)	Four Six Eight	7/8 yard 1 3/8 yards 1 3/8 yards	7/8 yard 7/8 yard 1 3/8 yards

Serging Tips

- Chain off at the corners. It's the fastest and easiest method. Serge finish the lengthwise grain edges first, then the crosswise grain. The lengthwise grain has less tendency to pull out at the corners where the edge finishing intersects. Dab seam sealant on the corners. Allow it to dry, then snip. We know a restaurant owner who has her 400 home-serged napkins laundered and pressed daily. After a year, she hasn't detected noticeable fraying at the corners. To avoid dog-eared corners, see page 103.

- Experiment with thread types. Woolly Nylon is our favorite choice because it spreads to cover a rolled edge beautifully, and minimizes fraying at the corners. Other thread types we like for finishing include: cotton-covered polyester; buttonhole twist; rayon thread, especially variegated; metallics for holiday table toppings; two strands of all-purpose or serger thread; or a "blended" combination of Woolly Nylon and all-purpose, serger, rayon, or metallic thread!

- Experiment with stitch types. Although a rolled edge (see page 96) remains the most popular and durable finish for cloth napkins, a balanced stitch is a refreshing look. Use buttonhole twist in both the upper and lower loopers.

Creative Napkin Ideas

- Line with coordinating or contrasting fabric. Serge edge finish as one layer. Lining is a clever way to tie together related, but not matching, prints and colors. Many of the Palmer/Pletsch Sewing Vacation students like to work with self-fabric so that the wrong side of a print won't show.

  Also, to strengthen edges, align crosswise and lengthwise edges. Rolled edges will be more uniform on all four sides, too.

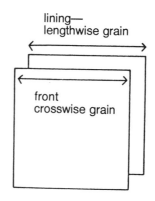

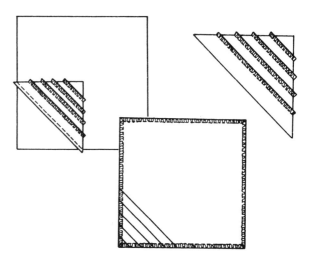

- Make strip patchwork napkins. Serge the strips together, then straight stitch the longest strip to the napkin, right sides together, as shown. Fold the strip triangle down, enclosing the seams. Serge finish the napkin edges.

- Have fun folding cloth napkins—even kids love to do it.

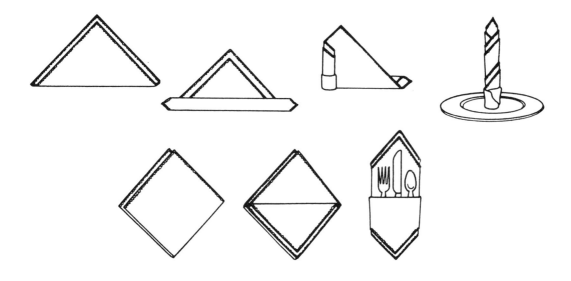

Placemats

Placemats are handy for everyday use an a snap to serge! Make a set to match your napkins. Only one yard of 45" wide fabric will yield six 14" x 16" placemats. Use your favorite ready-made placemat as a pattern.

Yardage estimates—Yardages are given for single thickness only and for 14" x 16" size. Double the yardage for reversible or lined placemats.

Quantity	Fabric Width	
	45"	54"
Four	1 yard	1 yard
Six	1 yard	1 yard
Eight	2 yards	1 1/2 yards

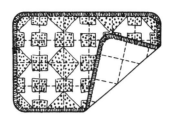

Fabric tips—Use double-sided quilted fabric for super-quick placemats. Just serge the edges and you're done! For firmer placemats, try these layering strategies:

Single-sided quilted fabric **plus** fusible web **plus** single-sided quilted fabric.

Single-sided quilted fabric **plus** fusible web **plus** fabric.

Fabric **plus** fleece plus **fabric** with fusible web between the layers.

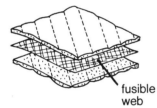

fusible web

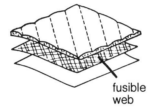

fusible web

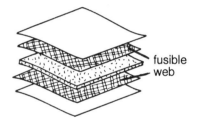

fusible web

All of the above can be channel quilted with conventional straight stitching or serged chainstitching.

Note: For fleece, we like bonded fiberfill like Thermo Lam or Pellon fleece.

Serging tips—Facilitate continuous serging by rounding off corners. Use a cup as a template. Trim with a rotary cutter, or cut placemats in an oval shape.

If fleece-filled placemats are too thick to feed into the knives smoothly, compress the layers first with a wide, long, conventional zigzag then serge edge finish.

Use the "belly button" rule—start serging in the center of the bottom edge of the placemat. Less-than-perfect lapping of the serging will be hidden under the dinner plate! For continuous, circular serging tips, see page 36.

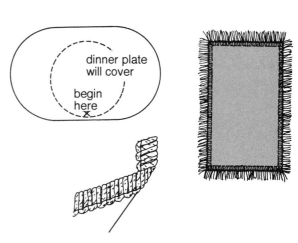

dinner plate will cover

begin here

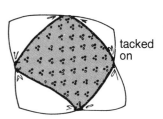

If you can't use a heavy thread in the lower looper, yet want the placemats to be reversible, wrap the edge. See page 30.

Make flatlocked and fringed placemats (see page 123). Choose loosely woven linen looks and put your television-watching troops to work fringing!

Thread types—Experiment with different threads. On heavier, multi-layer or quilted and stitched placemats, we like heavier threads such as pearl or crochet cotton, or topstitching thread used in both loopers with a wide, balanced stitch. On thinner, single layer placemats, try Woolly Nylon, all-purpose, and rayon threads in a medium width balanced stitch. A rolled edge can also be used, giving a unique look to lightweight placemats.

Pillows

Make tie-ons for square pillows. The tie-ons should be twice the pillow size (for example, a 16" pillow requires two 32" squares). Roll the edges of the squares and tie on, gathering the fabric into attractive folds. For smaller squares, simply hand tack corners to the pillow. These are great for preprinted motifs.

tied on

tacked on

Finish ruffles with a rolled edge. For extra body, make the ruffles double layered, using self-fabric or a contrasting color.

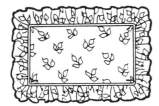

Make instant pillows! Serge the edges of each piece separately, then straight stitch them together 2" from the edge for a flanged look. Leave a 4" opening for stuffing.

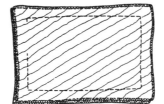

Flatlock fringe square fabric. Stitch the pieces together, leaving a 4" opening for the stuffing.

Quilts and Crafts

A version of vintage "crazy quilts" flatlocked patchwork simulates hand-worked feather embroidery stitches. Topstitching thread, fine yarn, and pearl cotton are recommended. Block quilts are the easiest and fastest to make.

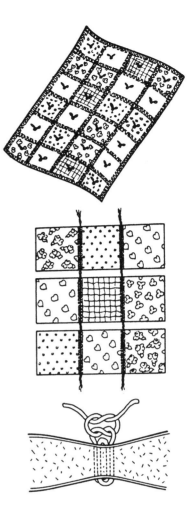

1. Plot the patchwork color scheme.

2. Flatlock all parallel rows in one direction.

3. Chain between blocks as shown. Then flatlock all the rows in the opposite direction, trimming off the chains between the rows.

4. Back with a lining, sandwiching batting between. (It may be necessary to compress layers first with a wide, long zigzag stitch.) Tuft through all layers and edge finish with decorative serging.

Use your quilted fabric for quilts, handbags, garments, doll accessories, and pillows. Let your imagination go!

Use Your Serger to Cut Strips

Transform your serger into a stripping machine! Remove the needles and thread; mark the desired width from the knife on the front guard plate. Align the fabric edge with this mark as you feed the fabric through the serger to cut strips. This stripping method is a welcome relief for hands tired from cutting yards and yards of rag baskets, rag knitting, "rag point," and braided rugs.

Creative Serging: Quick References and Handy Resources

The Love and Care of Your Serger

Keep It Clean

Lint quickly builds up under the throat plate and can clog knife blades, causing skipped stitches. If lint builds up on the thread guides, it can cause uneven threads feeding through the machine. Dust often with the soft brushes supplied with your machine or use ozone-safe, canned, compressed air. Attach the straw-like tube to the nozzle for the most powerful spraying action. Or, use the new mini-adapters on your vacuum hose to draw out lint build-up. A slightly oil-dampened stencil or paint brush works wonders when hunting down lint in serger cracks and crevices.

Oil as Necessary

Use an oil specially made for sergers. Check your manual for oiling points. Many machines need to be oiled after 8–10 hours of high speed serging. If your machine is making more noise than usual, it likely needs oil.

Note: Before oiling, read your manual and check with your dealer. Some new models require little or no oiling.

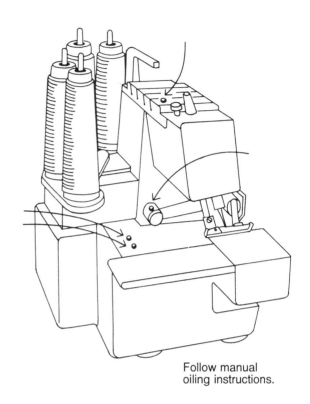

Follow manual oiling instructions.

Change Needles

Needles with sharp, smooth points are essential to care-free serging. If the needle is slightly dull or burred, it will cause a clicking noise and possibly skipped stitches. Synthetic fibers dull needles more quickly than natural fibers. Change the needle when skipped or irregular stitches occur. Sometimes changing to a different **size** needle improves stitching quality.

Note: Be certain you are using the right type and size needle. Some models demand a specific type of household or industrial needle. Also, the size range is generally limited to from 9–14. Stock up on those needles that work without fail, in a range of sizes.

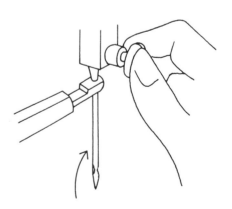

Replace dull or burred needles.

Change the Knife Blades

If you avoid cutting pins, your knives last much longer. When the trimmed edge is ragged, however, one or both blades may be dull. One is made of hard alloy steel and rarely needs changing. The other is softer so is usually the only one that will be dull or damaged. Thick fabrics and synthetics also dull blades faster. Check your manual to see which of the blades on your serger is the softer one (it will be the least expensive). **Replace** a dull blade, being sure it is inserted properly. If skeptical about your ability to remove and replace a knife properly, hire your dealer to do it.

Note: Serger knives cannot be resharpened like scissors with a "knife" edge. They cut because of the downward force of the two rectangular edges coming together.

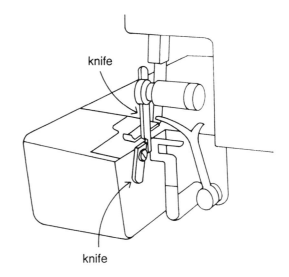

Follow manual instructions for changing knives.

Selecting the Proper Width, Length and Needle Size

Weight	Fabric Type	Width	Length	Needle Size
Light	Voile	2.5mm	2.0mm	12 (80)
	Gingham	3.5mm	2.5mm	12
	Georgette	1.5mm*	2.5mm	12
	Sheer	1.5mm*	2.5mm	12
	Lace	1.5mm*	2.0mm	12
	Silk & Silkies	2.5mm	2.5mm	12
Medium Woven	Poplin	4.0mm	3.0mm	12–14 (80 or 90)
	Gabardine	4.0mm	3.0mm	12–14
Medium Knit	Jersey	4.0mm	2.0mm	12–14
	T-shirting	4.0mm	2.0mm	12–14
	Double Knit	4.0mm	2.0mm	12–14
Heavy	Denim	5.0mm	2.0mm	14–16 (90–100)
	Terry Cloth	5.0mm	2.0mm	14–16
	Corduroy	5.0mm	2.5mm	14–16
	Velour	5.0mm	2.5mm	14–16
	Wools	4.5mm	3.0mm	12–14

* Rolled Hem width

Troubleshooting

Problem	Solutions	
Skipped Stitches	• Replace a bent, dull, or damaged needle. • Use the correct type and size needle for the serger, fabric, and thread. • Thread correctly, through all guides and eyes. Thread can easily come out of the open thread guides. The looper or needle tension may be too tight. Loosen one then the other to see which works.	• Change needle size. • Increase the presser foot pressure for heavier fabrics. • Insert needle correctly. The eye of the needle must face exactly toward the front of the machine.
Puckered Fabric	• Adjust differential feed to below 1. • Loosen needle thread tension. • Adjust foot pressure.	• Check for correct threading. • Shorten the stitch length. • Check for correct cutting from the knives.
Excessive Stretching	• Adjust differential feed to above 1. • Lighten the foot pressure. • Be careful not to stretch fabric as you sew. • Serge in from the edge, trim off at least 1/4".	• Stabilize edge (see pages 41-42). • Lengthen stitch.
Irregular Stitches	• Thread correctly. • Replace with new or different size needle. • Check for proper cutting action of knives. • Change to the correct size needle for thread or fabric. *Note:* If the texture of the fabric is uneven, irregular stitches will occur. It is difficult to compensate for this.	• Insert needle correctly. • Adjust tension. • Thread must feed from the spool smoothly.
Fabric Doesn't Feed Well	• Presser foot is up. • Clean lint out of feed dogs. • Increase or decrease foot pressure depending on fabric weight.	• Lengthen the stitch. • Check knife blades for excessive wear.
Thread is Breaking	• Balance the tension settings. • Insert needle correctly. • Change the needle. • Try a jeans or topstitching needle with a larger eye. • Rethread machine in proper threading order.	• Use a high-quality thread. • Loosen tension on the breaking thread. • Check for thread caught on spool notch, thread stand, or guides on machine.
Needle Breaks	• Change to a new needle. • Change to a larger size needle. • Avoid excessive pulling of the fabric while serging	• Insert the needle correctly. • Check for thread caught in a thread guide.
Machine Jams	• Engage moveable knife. • Pull thread tails to the back as you begin to serge. • Make sure fabric trimmings fall away from, not into, the serger. • Check for proper cutting position of knives.	• Close protective front cover while serging. • Lengthen stitch, especially if using heavy threads. • Serge fewer layers of fabric or compress thick layers.
Seam Pulls Open to Expose Stitches	• Tighten the needle tension, or • Make sure thread is engaged in the tension dials.	• Loosen the lower looper tension. • Use wooly nylon thread in the needle.
Excessive Machine Noise	• Clean and oil machine. • Consult your dealer if problem persists. *Note:* Check to see if the surface that the machine is sitting on is making the noise.	• Insert new needle.
Trimmed Edge Is Ragged	• Reset knife blades correctly • Allow machine to trim away at leat 1/8" of off the fabric edge	• Change to a new knife blade, or engage movable knife

Sought-After Serger Feet & Accessories

"Serging with your feet" is an increasingly popular activity. More and more enthusiasts are looking for ways to stretch the utilitarian and creative capabilities of their sergers, and have realized that having the right feet can make the difference. When purchasing a new serger, ask what feet are standard, what are optional, and if there are any other generic or branded feet that will fit. If you already own a serger, call your dealer occasionally for an update on what new feet are available. Once you've purchased a foot, experiment! Undoubtedly you'll devise new timesaving and creative uses in addition to those mentioned here.

Many of the new serger feet are snap-on. Don't worry if your model uses shank-style feet; your dealer probably has a snap-on adapter available. Also, not all the feet shown are compatible with all models, and although the finished technique may look the same, the configuration of the foot or attachment used will likely vary brand-to-brand, and possibly model-to-model.

Some Cautions: Remember, only certain branded or generic feet are interchangeable among brands, and even then, may be limited to specific models. If in doubt about the suitability of a foot, buy it with a return guarantee, follow the instructions, and test-serge with care, removing any needle(s) necessary, and turning the handwheel to advance the stitch.

Narrow-rolled hem foot. For narrow-rolled or balanced finishing and/or finishing or seaming; the stitch is formed over the narrower, shorter stitch finger. Some new models do not require changing to a special foot for narrow serging. May require a special plate, also.

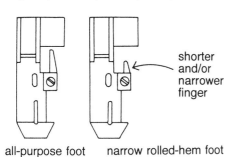

shorter and/or narrower finger

all-purpose foot   narrow rolled-hem foot

Transparent chainstitch foot. For serged chainstitching; the clear foot allows viewing the stitch as you serge. Also, handy for shirring, using elastic thread in the chainstitch looper.

serged chainstitch

Blindhem foot. For serged blindhemming. Some are available in different sizes for different thicknesses of fabric. Also, works well for guiding the fabric when flatlocking, or for any time serging without trimming is desired.

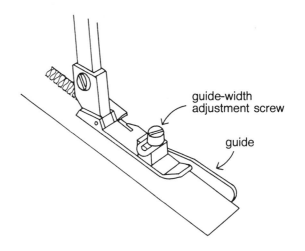

guide-width adjustment screw

guide

Elastic/taping foot, elastic guide feet or "elasticator." For regulating the amount of elastic stretch while it is being applied. Also can be used for applying narrow ribbon or trims.

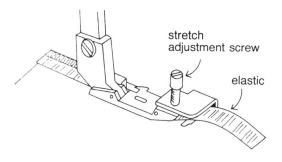

stretch adjustment screw

elastic

Cording or gimp foot. For precise serged application of cording or gimp. Different sizes may be available for different size cording or finer gimp. Also can be used to apply fine wire or fishing line.

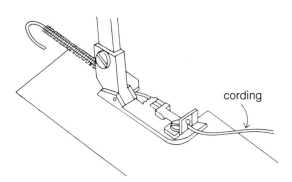

cording

Lace-sewing foot. For ultra-narrow seaming and finishing of lace and trim insertions, so popular for heirloom serging (pages 105-109).

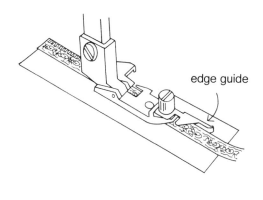

edge guide

Piping foot. For uniform, smooth insertion of piping in a serged seam. (The piping is guided through a groove in the bottom of the foot. Also, for making piping trim. Sometimes called a "cording" foot.)

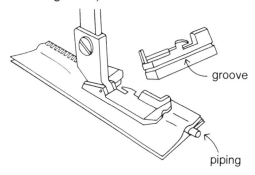

groove

piping

Ribbon-sewing foot. For "hands-free" serged application of narrow, ribbon or trim. Some standard serger feet integrate ribbon-application capability.

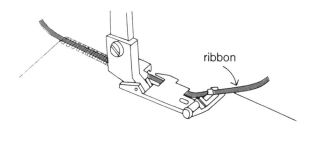

ribbon

Bias tape guide/piping foot. For creating and inserting piping in a serged seam. Also, for making piping trim. (Refer to the **Cloth guide attachment** on page 148 for cutting the bias strips.)

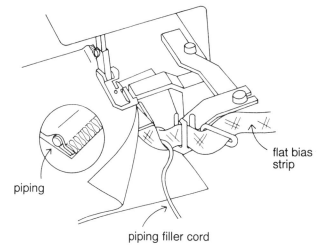

flat bias strip

piping

piping filler cord

Bias binder attachment. For making and applying bias binding; the flat bias strip is folded around the edge, and secured with serged chainstitching. (Refer to the **Cloth guide attachment** below for cutting the bias strips.)

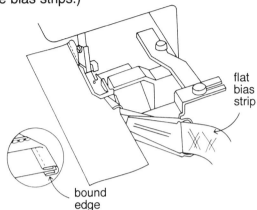

flat bias strip

bound edge

Shirring, gathering, or ruffling foot. For gathering of the lower layer while serging it to the flat top layer. Used in combination with differential feeding.

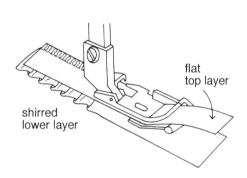

flat top layer

shirred lower layer

Gathering plate. Like the fabric separator, for gathering of the lower layer while serging to the flat top layer. Also used in combination with differential.

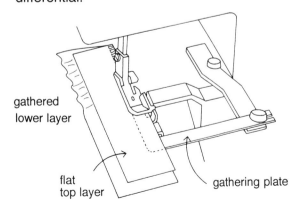

gathered lower layer

flat top layer

gathering plate

Pearl/sequin or beading foot. For easy, smooth application of bead strands. The strand is fed through channels under the back and over the front of the foot. Also works well for applying sequins, heavy wire, cording, and fishing line.

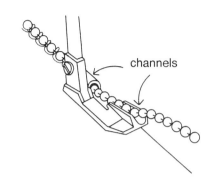

channels

Fabric separator attachment. Also for gathering of the lower layer while serging to the flat top layer. Used in combination with differential feeding.

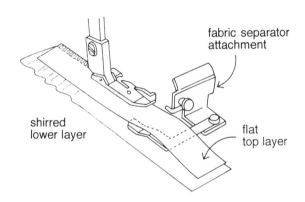

fabric separator attachment

shirred lower layer

flat top layer

Cloth guide attachment. For gauging even seam allowances and cutting even-width strips of fabric.

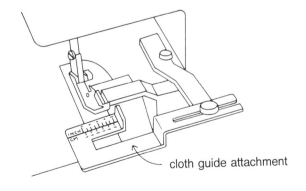

cloth guide attachment

HELPFUL SERGER NOTIONS

Some of these notions come as standard accessories with your serger, but all of them can also be purchased separately. Here's what they're used for:

Auxiliary lights—For more light. Some fasten directly to the serger. Also available are flexible arm lights that fasten to the table.

Basting Tape—Regular and water-soluble basing tapes hold fabrics like slinky, and silk likes in place while serging.

Compressed Air—Keeps your serger lint-free. Be sure to use an ozone-friendly brand. Note: Some repair specialists now recommend against using compressed air. Check with your dealer.

Dust Covers—To minimize dust build-up.

Extension Table—Creates a flat surface around the serging area.

Glue Stick—Temporarily bastes seams and trims for easier serging. Washable.

Lint Brush—For quick cleaning of small areas. An oil dampened stencil brush also works well.

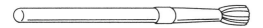

Loop Turner—For burying thread tails under serging.

Looper Threader—Long curved threader perfect for threading any needle or looper eye with any thread.

Magnetic Seam Guide-Attaches to the knife cover as a guide for accurate serging. Movable to trim various widths.

Magnifying Lens—Attaches to the front of your serger for magnifying threading and stitching.

Melt-adhesive or Fusible Thread—Such as Thread Fuse or stitch 'n Fuse, for fuse-basting serged stitches.

Needles, Inserters, and Threaders—Assists in inserting or threading needle(s). The new "Perfect Threader" from Australia also becomes a needle inserter.

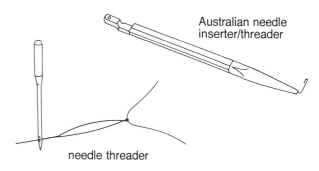

Australian needle inserter/threader

needle threader

Needle Nose Pliers or Needle Grippers—For easy, straight insertion of serger needles.

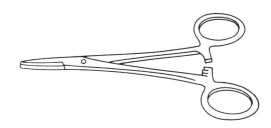

Needles for Sergers—Have lots of sizes for your serger on hand. Your serger can be damaged if the wrong type or size needle is used. See your manual or ask your dealer.

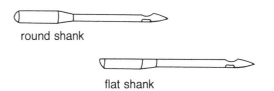

round shank

flat shank

Rotary Cutter and Cutting Mat—Cut out fast! Both available in a variety of sizes.

Screw Driver—For changing needles, knives, and on some sergers, stitch setting. Standard equipment with most sergers but replacement sizes are available.

Seam Guide—A self-adhesive decal that is placed on the looper cover for easy gauging of seam width.

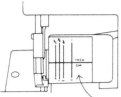

Seam Ripper—Rip any serged seam quickly. Look for the new surgical types that easily slide under the looper threads.

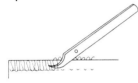

Seam Sealant—Liquid plastic like Dritz Fray Check, Allen's Stop Fraying, or Plaid's No-Fray that secures stitches. Super for corners.

Serger Knives—Work together to rim the fabric. Replacement for the softer knife comes with your serger, or can be purchased, as can the more expensive steel alloy knife.

Serger Foot Pedal Mat—Slotted rubber mat prevents pedal from sliding.

Serger Stops—A pad that is placed under your serger to stop it from moving on the table top.

Spool Caps—Caps that prevent catching thread in the conventional spool thread slit. (These are generally standard accessories, but can be purchased separately.)

Stitch References—Special cards or dials used for recording and referencing thread types, needle sizes, tension settings, and optional feet.

Tapestry or Double-Eyed Needle—A rounded point needle ideal for burying tail chains under your stitching.

Thread Inventory—Should include a range of regular, utilitarian, and decorative threads (see Chapter 3, pages 13-19) so you're ready to serge!

Thread Nets—Prevent slippery threads from dropping off the spool or cone while serging.

Thread Holders and Stands—
Hold coned or decorative thread behind the serger, or on the thread rod.

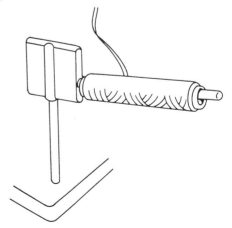

Thread Racks—For neat, compact storage of coned and tubed threads.

Tote Bags—Indispensable for care-free transporting. Not a standard serger accessory. Both hard and soft carrying cases available.

Trim Catchers—Handy accessories that sit under your serger, or attach to the front legs, and catch all those messy clippings. Some have a non-slip back to keep your serger in place.

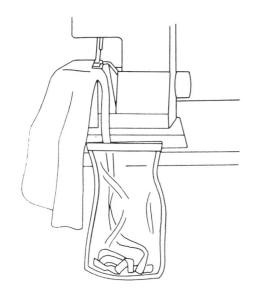

Vacuum Attachments—Mini-adapters scale down a standard vacuum hose, so it can be used to clean out hard-to-reach areas.

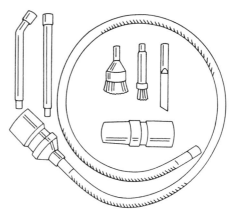

Washable Markers—Substituted for notches when serging. Either water- or air-erasable.

Creative Serging Sources

Finding a Dealer

It's likely you already depend on a serger dealer in your area. In not, refer to the Yellow Pages of the phone book, under "Sewing Machines, Household-Dealers," where retailers are listed by store name and sometimes by machine-brand-name. Remember, some dealers are departments within a fabric store, and some fabric stores also sell machines.

Serger companies (see the Acknowledgments) will also refer you to local dealers. Even if there's not a dealer in your town, there's probably one in the next closest metropolitan area.

What a Good Dealer Offers

A knowledgeable, enthusiastic dealer can be instrumental in helping maximize your serger investment. Some of the many services they offer:

- On-the-spot advice.

- Serger classes and clubs.

- Videos, books, manuals and workbooks.

- Brand-specific periodicals designed to show creative serging applications.

- Sponsorship of special educational events.

- Source for serger needles, parts, specialty (and often hard-to-find) threads and other helpful notions.

- When driving is impossible, convenient phone-order shopping for needles, parts, threads and notions. (Most will gladly mail or ship to you.)

- Reliable and readily accessible, factory-authorized repair and maintenance services.

- Sales of new and used sergers; trade-in options.

We appreciate these services, and the difference they can make in our readers' serging satisfaction; we urge you to consider the range and quality of these services, rather than judge dealerships solely on their merchandise pricing.

Organizations, Periodicals, References

Note: Chilton publishes several bestselling serger books (see page 135). Ask for them wherever you purchased this book, or fabric stores or bookstores.

American Sewing Guild, P.O. Box 8476, Medford, OR 97504 (503) 772-4059. Network with others who love serging, sewing, quilting and crafts. Contact about chapters in your area.

The Creative Machine, P.O. Box 2634-B, Menlo Park, CA 94026. Talk to the serger and sewing authors and authorities. Subscription, $12 (quarterly).

The Creative Needle, 1 Apollo Road, Lookout Mountain, GA 30750. Emphasis on machine arts, heirloom sewing and children's projects. Bimonthly, $19/year.

National 4-H Council, 7100 Connecticut Ave., Chevy Chase MD 20815-4999. Call your county extension office for local 4-H information.

On-line computer services, such as America Online, Compuserve, The Crafts BB, Genie, National Videotex and Prodigy, offer sewing forums full of serging advice. Ask about signing on at your local computer dealer, and look for related articles in sewing publications.

Palmer/Pletsch Associates, P.O. Box 12046, Portland, OR (800) 728-3784. Serger books, videos, seminars, workshops and teacher training. (Also, see listing on page 153.) Call or write for information.

Serger Update, P.O. Box 5026, Harlan, IA 51537 (800) 444-0454. Devoted exclusively to serging news and techniques; no advertising. Monthly newsletter, $48/year (watch for promotional discounts in Sew News).

Sewing Update, P.O. Box 5026, Harlan IA 51537 (800) 444-0454. The latest sewing tips and trends, fully illustrated in a concise format. No advertising. Bimonthly newsletter, $24/year (watch for promotional discounts in Sew News).

Sew News, P.O. Box 3134, Harlan, IA 51537-3134 (800) 289-6397. Comprehensive, monthly sewing news. Look for Ann Price's "Machines in Motion" column and serger-related ads. $15.97/year.

Sewer's Source Letter, CraftSource, 7509 7th Pl SW, Seattle, WA 98106. Quarterly review of mail-order sources. $18/year.

Threads, 63 South Main St., P.O. Box 5506, Newtown, CT 06470-9977. Beautifully presented coverage of serging, sewing, fiber arts and needle crafts. Six issues/year—$26.

Professional Association of Custom Clothiers (PACC), 1375 Broadway, New York, NY 10018 (201) 302-2150. National trade association for pros in sewing- or serging-related businesses.

Why We've Included Catalog Sources

Note: As you know, we encourage support of your local fabric retailer, serger dealer, or department. But we also realize that many of you live in remote areas, where speciality threads and notions simply are not available. So, we've compiled this list of established mail-order companies. If we've neglected to include your favorites, or if service from any of these is questionable, please let us know. (There are many more reliable suppliers, but due to space limitations, we focused on those specializing in serging supplies.)

Key: "LSASE" means long, self-addressed, stamped envelope.

Aardvark Adventures, P.O. Box 2449, Livermore, CA 94551, (415) 443-2687. Decorative serging threads and yarns, including metallics. Entertaining newspaper/catalog, $2 (refundable).

A Great Notion Sewing Supply, Ltd., 13847-17A Ave., White Rock, BC V4A 7H4, Canada, (604) 538-2829. Hard-to-find sewing supplies. Catalog, $1.

Baer Fabrics, 515 E. Market St., Louisville, KY 40202, (800) 788-2237. Fabrics and notions galore. Call for details.

Britex Fabrics, 146 Geary St., San Francisco, CA 94108, (415) 392-2910. Designer and unusual fabrics. Personalized swatching service, $5.

Clotilde, Inc., 1909 SW First Ave., Ft. Lauderdale, FL 33315, (800) 772-2891. Special serger threads and notions, plus thousands of sewing items. Free color catalog.

The Cutting Edge, Box 397, St. Peters, MO 63376. Serger threads-all-purpose and decorative (including Success acrylic yarn), related notions, patterns by Cindy Cummins (see pages 57 and 59) and books. Catalog, $1 (refundable with order).

G Street Fabrics Mail Order Service, 12240 Wilkins Ave., Rockville, MD 20852, (800) 333-9191. Extensive fabric notion and book offerings. Notion list free, custom samples, $5.

Hancock Fabrics, 3841 Hinkleville Rd., Paducah, KY 42001 (800) 626-2723, ext. 456. LSASE.

Herrschners, Hoover Rd., Stevens Point, WI 54492, (800) 441-0838. Serger books and notions. Free color catalog.

Home-Sew, Bethlehem, PA 18018. Sewing and serger notions. Free catalog.

Nancy's Notions, Ltd., P.O. Box 683, Beaver Dam, WI 53916, (800) 833-0690. Serger threads, tools, books and accessories, plus a wide range of general sewing notions. Also, ask about their video catalog and club. Free color catalog.

National Thread & Supply, 695 Red Oak Rd., Stockbridge, GA 30281, (800) 847-1001, ext 1688; in GA, (404) 389-9115. Name-brand sewing supplies and notions. Free catalog.

Newark Dressmaker Supply, P.O. Box 2448, Lehigh Valley, PA 18001, (215) 837-7500). Serger notions and threads. Free catalog.

Northwest Sewing, P.O. Box 25826, Seattle, WA 98115, (800) 745-5739. Free decorative-thread catalog.

Oregon Tailor Supply, P.O. Box 42284, Portland, OR 97242, (800) 678-2457. Coned thread and other notions. LSASE.

Palmer/Pletsch Associates, P.O. Box 12046, Portland, OR 97212, (800) 728-3784. Books, videos, specialty threads, and notions. Call or write for information.

Sew-Art International, P.O. Box 550, Bountiful, UT 84011, (800) 231-ARTS. Decorative threads and supplies. Free catalog.

Sew/Fit Co., P.O. Box 565, La Grange, IL 60525, (708) 579-3252. Serger notions, cutting tools, and mats. Free color catalog.

Sewing Emporium, 1079 Third Ave., Chula Vista, CA 92010, (619) 420-3490. Serger needles, notions, books, furniture. Catalog, $4.95 (refundable).

Sew-Knit Distributors, 9789 Florida Blvd., Baton Rouge, LA 70815, (800) BUY-KNIT or (504) 923-1285. Generic and branded serger feet and accessories. Call or send LSASE with request, specifying serger brand and model.

The Sewing Place, 18770 Cox Ave., Saratoga, CA 95070. Serger needles and feet, plus books by Gale Grigg Hazen. Specify your brand and model if ordering machine accessories. LSASE for free information.

Speed Stitch, 3113-D Broadpoint Dr., Harbor Heights, FL 33983, (800) 8744115. Serging threads (including Sulky), notions and books. Catalog, $3 (refundable).

Treadleart, 25834 Narbonne Ave., Suite I, Lomita, CA 90717 (800) 3274222. Serging supplies, notions, decorative threads, and inspiration. Catalog, $1.50.

YLI Corporation, 482 N. Freedom Blvd., Provo, UT 84601, (800) 854-1932. Decorative, specialty, serger, and all-purpose threads, yarns, and ribbons. Catalog, $2.50.

Other Books Available From Chilton

Contemporary Quilting Series

Applique the Ann Boyce Way, by Ann Boyce

Contemporary Quilting Techniques, by Pat Cairns

Fast Patch, by Anita Hallock

Fourteen Easy Baby Quilts, by Margaret Dittman

Machine-Quilted Jackets, Vests, and Coats, by Nancy Moore

Precision Pieced Quilts Using the Foundation Method, by Jane Hall and DIxie Haywood

The Quilter's Guide to Rotary Cutting, by Donna Poster

Quilts by the Slice, by Beckie Olson

Scrap Quilts Using Fast Patch, by Anita Hallock

Speed-Cut Quilts, by Donna Poster

Super Simple Quilts, by Kathleen Eaton

Teach Yourself Machine Piecing and Quilting, by Debra Wagner

Three-Dimensional Applique, by Jodie Davis

Craft Kaleidoscope Series

Fabric Painting Made Easy, by Nancy Ward

How to Make Cloth Books for Children, by Anee Pellowski

Creative Machine Arts Series

ABCs of Serging, by Tammy Young and Lori Bottom

The Button Lover's Book, by Marilyn Green

Claire Shaeffer's Fabric Sewing Guide

The Complete Book of Machine Embrodiery, by Robbie and Tony Fanning

Creative Nurseries Illustrated, by Debra Terry and Juli Plooster

Creative Serging Illustrated, by Pati Palmer, Gail Brown, and Sue Green

Distinctive Serger Gifts and Crafts, by Naomi Baker and Tammy Young

The Fabric Lover's Scrapbook, by Margaret Dittman

Friendship Quilts by Hand and Machine, by Carolyn Vosburg Hall

Gifts Galore, by Jane Warnick and Jackie Dodson

How to Make Soft Jewelry, by Jackie Dodson

Innovative Serging, by Gail Brown and Tammy Young

Innovative Sewing, by Gail Brown and Tammy Young

Instant Interiors by Gail Brown

Owner's Guide to Sewing Machines, Sergers, and Knitting Machines, by Gale Grigg Hazen

Petite Pizzazz, by Barb Griffin

Putting on the Glitz, by Sandra L. Hatch and Ann Boyce

Quick Napkin Creations by Gail Brown

Serged Garments in Minutes, by Tammy Young and Naomi Baker

Sew Sensational Gifts, by Naomi Baker and Tammy Young

Sew, Serge, Press, by Jan Saunders
Sewing and Collecting Vintage Fashions, by Eileen MacIntosh
Simply Serge Any Fabric, by Naomi Baker and Tammy Young
Soft Gardens: Make Flowers with Your Sewing Machine, by Yvonne Perez-Collins
Twenty Easy Machine-Made Rugs, by Jackie Dodson

Know Your Sewing Machine Series, by Jackie Dodson
Know Your Bernina, second edition
Know Your Brother, with Jane Warnick
Know Your Elna, with Carol Ahles
Know Your New Home, with Judi Cull and Vicki Lyn Hastings
Know Your Pfaff, with Audrey Griese
Know Your Sewing Machine
Know Your Singer
Know Your Viking, with Jan Saunders
Know Your White, with Jan Saunders

Know Your Serger Series, by Tammy Young and Naomi Baker
Know Your Baby Lock
Know Your Pfaff Hobbylock
Know Your Serger
Know Your White Superlock

Teach Yourself to Sew Better Series, by Jan Saunders
A Step-by-Step Guide to Your Bernina
A Step-by-Step Guide to Your New Home
A Step-by-Step Guide to Your Sewing Machine
A Step-by-Step Guide to Your Viking

Metric Conversions	
1/8" = 3 mm	1/8 yd = .12 m
1/4" = 6 mm	1/4 yd = .23 m
3/8" = 10 mm or 1 cm	3/8 yd = .35 m
1/2" = 13 mm or 1.3 cm	1/2 yd = .46 m
5/8" = 15 mm or 1.5 cm	5/8 yd = .58 m
3/4" = 20 mm or 2 cm	3/4 yd = .69 m
1" = 25 mm or 2.5 cm	1 yd = .92 m

Index